W9-CNC-633

CHOLESTEROL

NOTE

This publication was written by a registered dietitian to provide insights into better eating habits to promote health and wellness. It does not provide a cure for any specific ailment or condition and is not a substitute for the advice and/or treatment given by a licensed physician.

First published in French in 2014 by Les Publications Modus Vivendi Inc. under the title *Cholestérol*.
© Alexandra Leduc and Les Publications Modus Vivendi Inc., 2017.

MODUS VIVENDI PUBLISHING INC.
55 Jean-Talon Street West
Montreal, Quebec H2R 2W8
CANADA

modusvivendipublishing.com

Publisher: Marc G. Alain
Editorial director: Isabelle Jodoin
Content and copy editor: Nolwenn Gouezel
English-language editor: Carol Sherman
Translator: Donna Vekteris
English-language copy editor: Maeve Haldane
Graphic designers: Émilie Houle and Gabrielle Lecomte
Food photographer: André Noël (anoelphoto.com)
Food stylist: Gabrielle Dalessandro
Additional photography:
Pages 6, 18, 20, 47, 48, 49, 50, 51, 52, 53, 54, 55, 56, 57, 59, 60, 61, 62, 63, 64, 65, 66, 67, 70, 72, 80, 85, 86, 90, 94, 96, 102, 106, 108, 111, 114, 122, 124, 131, 138, 147, 150, 152, 154, 162, 165: Dreamstime.com
Pages 5, 8, 12, 15, 17, 23, 25, 29, 31, 32, 35, 37, 38, 41, 43, 54, 56, 58, 65, 74, 120, 166: iStock

ISBN: 978-1-77286-050-4 (PAPERBACK)

ISBN: 978-1-77286-051-1 (PDF)
ISBN: 978-1-77286-052-8 (EPUB)
ISBN: 978-1-77286-053-5 (KINDLE)

Legal deposit — Bibliothèque and Archives nationales du Québec, 2017
Legal deposit — Library and Archives Canada, 2017

All rights reserved. No part of this publication may be reproduced, stored in a retrieval system or transmitted, in any form or by any means, without the publisher's written authorization.

Government of Quebec – Tax Credit for Book Publishing – Program administered by SODEC

Funded by the Government of Canada

Printed in Canada

KNOW
WHAT
TO
EAT

CHOLESTEROL
21 DAYS OF MENUS

Alexandra Leduc, RD

MODUS VIVENDI

CONTENTS

High cholesterol is not a disease in itself, but rather a metabolic condition that can be controlled to some degree through good eating habits and a healthy lifestyle. Cholesterolemia refers to the amount of cholesterol in the blood that makes it possible to evaluate one's "cholesterol count." Hypercholesterolemia refers to an abnormally high level of cholesterol.

Hypercholesterolemia, or high cholesterol, is said to be a silent condition, because most of the time there are no symptoms associated with it. This does not make it any less dangerous, however. It is a major risk factor for cardiac problems and strokes.

This book is designed to encourage you to make better food choices and easily adopt a cholesterol-lowering diet with the aim of improving your lipid profile. This will help you to avoid the complications associated with high cholesterol and boost your overall health.

Cholesterol is a lipid in the sterol family. Its name is composed of the prefix "chole," from the Greek *chole*, which means "bile," and the suffix "sterol," from the Greek *stereos*, which means "solid." Cholesterol was first discovered in 1758 by French chemist François Poulletier de la Salle, who found the substance in gallstones. It was only in 1814, however, that his counterpart Michel Eugène Chevreul coined the term "cholesterine."

For the longest time cholesterol suffered from a bad reputation. We now know, however, that not all cholesterol is harmful. In fact, it is essential for the proper functioning of the body, and we could not live without it!

So what is cholesterol? Is it fair to say that there is "good" cholesterol and "bad" cholesterol? Let's start with a short course in biology before we deal with the subject of high cholesterol — its causes and risk factors, symptoms, consequences and recommendations.

BIOLOGY 101

Cholesterol is a type of fat that is naturally present in the body. Cholesterol helps build cell membranes, plays an important role in the production of bile salts (essential to digestion) and ensures the synthesis of certain hormones. It is also essential for the synthesis of vitamin D, which helps calcium adhere to bones.

Cholesterol is mainly synthesized by the liver, which provides about two thirds of the cholesterol present in the body. The other third comes from diet. All foods containing animal fats (meat, processed meats, offal, butter, dairy products, eggs) contain cholesterol in varying amounts.

Cholesterol is soluble in fat but not water; as a result, it does not dissolve in the blood. To reach the cells, it circulates in the blood vessels through two types of transporters: LDL (low-density lipoprotein), which is commonly called "bad cholesterol," and HDL (high-density lipoprotein), commonly known as "good cholesterol." Strictly speaking, there is no such thing as "good" or "bad" cholesterol. Rather, LDL and HDL have two distinct purposes. The body needs both HDL and LDL. LDLs transport cholesterol from the liver to the organs via blood circulation. HDLs transport excess cholesterol accumulated in the cells and blood vessels to the liver, which in turn transforms it and eliminates it as waste. HDLs thus help the body eliminate excess fat.

The expression "to make cholesterol" suggests that something is abnormal. What it means most often is that the LDL level is too high. When produced in too-large quantities, LDLs cause an excessive amount of cholesterol to circulate in the arteries. Cholesterol gradually accumulates on the walls of the blood vessels and arteries, forming plaque. This condition is called atherosclerosis (see *The Consequences of High Cholesterol*, p. 14). It is also possible that the level of HDL transporters is not high enough, which can also cause health risks.

For information purposes, here are a few objectives to aim for, depending on your case.

	WITHOUT RISK FACTOR	WITH PRESENCE OF RISK FACTORS (tobacco, alcohol, hypertension, obesity, heredity, heart attack, etc.)
LDL	Rate under 5.0 mmol/l	Rate under 2.0 mmol/l
HDL	• Rate over 1.0 mmol/l in men • Rate over 1.3 mmol/l in women	• Rate over 1.0 mmol/l in men • Rate over 1.3 mmol/l in women
Total Cholesterol	Rate under 5.2 mmol/l	Rate under 5.2 mmol/l
Total Cholesterol/ HDL Cholesterol Ratio	Low risk of cardiovascular disease when under 6	Low risk of cardiovascular disease when under 4

HIGH CHOLESTEROL CAUSES AND RISK FACTORS

Contrary to popular belief, excess cholesterol is not only due to a diet too rich in fat, but also to genetic predisposition, diseases, certain medications and lifestyle.

Many different factors cause high cholesterol:

- primary hypercholesterolemia, usually genetic in origin, with abnormally elevated production of cholesterol;

- secondary hypercholesterolemia, which can be linked to a diet rich in saturated fatty acids, obesity, inactivity, excessive alcohol consumption and some diseases such as hypothyroidism and diabetes. It is also associated with the use of certain medications such as corticoids (for example, prescribed to fight acne or following a transplant), and some diuretics.

The non-modifiable risk factors are:

- age (blood cholesterol levels rise mainly after the age of 50 in men and after 60 in women);
- gender (men are more likely to be affected than women);
- family history.

The modifiable risk factors are:

- smoking (tobacco is a factor in atherosclerosis; it increases the risk of complications if combined with hypercholesterolemia);
- diet;
- obesity;
- alcohol consumption;
- inactivity (regular physical activity raises the level of good cholesterol and lowers the level of bad cholesterol).

HIGH CHOLESTEROL SYMPTOMS

In most cases, high cholesterol does not present any unpleasant symptoms until serious complications arise. In fact, most of the time it is a silent disease, which means that people who have a high LDL rate do not physically sense it. This is why the only way to determine one's blood cholesterol level is to have a blood analysis. A few signs, such as fatigue during exertion, however, may help raise suspicions.

It is generally recommended that you establish your lipid profile starting at age 40 for men, and around age 50 for women. But you should talk to your doctor about testing your cholesterol after age 20 if you have any risk factors present. Do not wait for the risk of high cholesterol to increase before taking your health in hand. Whatever your age, healthy habits are a key to keeping you well.

THE CONSEQUENCES OF HIGH CHOLESTEROL

An excessive amount of cholesterol can be deposited on the walls of arteries, for example on the arteries of the heart or the blood vessels of the brain. Over time, plaque forms, which grows over the years if high cholesterol is not treated. The plaque formed by the deposits can slow down blood flow or even obstruct the arteries. This process of the hardening of the arteries is called atherosclerosis.

The complications associated with high cholesterol include blood circulatory problems, pain in the legs, cardiovascular disease, heart attack and stroke. These complications are irreversible and will seriously affect your health and physical condition. They should not be taken lightly.

GENERAL RECOMMENDATIONS

High cholesterol can be avoided in part through a healthy lifestyle. Numerous studies show that quitting smoking, regular physical activity, improved weight management and a balanced diet help reduce the risks of high cholesterol.

QUITTING SMOKING

It is strongly recommended that you quit smoking. Tobacco is a major risk factor for cardiovascular disease, especially because it reduces the level of good cholesterol in the blood.

PHYSICAL ACTIVITY

Regular physical activity helps keep bones and muscles healthy as you age. It also helps you to stabilize your weight, control hunger and more easily identify the feeling of satiety. Physical activity has a positive effect on overall health while aiding with weight management.

To reduce the risk of high cholesterol, it is recommended that you engage in a cardiovascular activity for 30 to 45 minutes, three times a week. Walking fast, riding a bicycle and taking aerobics classes are all examples of good activities. Cardiovascular activity helps keep the heart healthy, reduces blood pressure and helps control blood cholesterol levels.

It is also recommended that you do light physical activity for at least 30 minutes a day. Gardening, walking, doing yoga, laundry and housework are all examples of light activities that are easily accessible.

Leave your car behind for short trips, travel on foot, routinely take the stairs even when there is an elevator, and sign up for Zumba classes (rhythmic class that features Latin-American music), for example. Move regularly and find activities you enjoy that will keep you motivated.

LOSING WEIGHT

Excess weight, especially in the abdominal area, is known to increase the risk of cardiovascular problems and high cholesterol. However, losing weight at all costs, by following a drastic diet, for example, will do more harm than good. It is important to adopt good habits and especially not to get into an endless cycle of dieting. A balanced diet and regular physical activity will help you stay healthy even if your weight is a little higher than normal. Losing 5 to 10 percent of your weight is known to have a major impact on health. It isn't necessary to aim for drastic weight loss when only a few pounds can make a big difference.

To help manage your weight, see the *Find Your Nutritional Balance* recommendation on page 20.

GOOD EATING HABITS

Eating well involves choosing the right ingredients, preparing them well and knowing when to eat them. In the following chapter, you will find dietery recommendations to help you more easily control your blood cholesterol levels.

High blood cholesterol levels can often be corrected or improved by changing your diet, and a good diet may help you avoid medical treatment.

Contrary to popular belief, it is not only dietary cholesterol that you have to watch out for, but saturated and trans fats, which are known to have a negative effect on blood cholesterol. No food is strictly forbidden — it is mainly a matter of eliminating your bad habits and adopting a healthy and balanced diet over the long term.

To benefit from a cholesterol-lowering diet, follow the recommendations in this chapter. They are mainly designed to help control your cholesterol, but can also be followed as a preventive measure.

RECOMMENDATIONS:

1. Find Your Nutritional Balance

2. Reduce Your Overall Fat Intake

3. Choose Good Fats

4. Reduce Bad Fats

5. Increase Your Fiber Consumption

6. Choose Plant Protein

7. Eat Less Refined Sugar

8. Moderate Your Sodium Intake

9. Reduce Your Alcohol Consumption

1 FIND YOUR NUTRITIONAL BALANCE

By following these tips, you will benefit from a healthy, balanced diet that will help you more easily manage your weight. These are good eating habits that everyone should follow.

- Eat three small meals per day at set times. If needed, add three snacks (in the morning, afternoon and evening). It is better not to overload the body. Three meals and three snacks (consisting of fruits, raw vegetables, nuts and seeds, yogurt or soy milk, for example) help provide a steady amount of energy throughout the day, which will help you avoid uncontrolled snacking and cravings. Do not, however, skip meals. Eating at set times will also give you more energy and help you manage your weight.

- Eat a balanced diet at each meal.

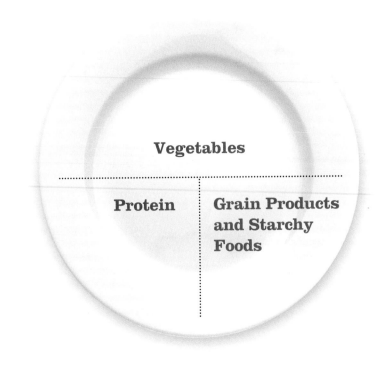

Take the time to prepare a balanced meal at lunchtime and dinnertime. Choose a source of protein that is low in fat to fill one quarter of your plate. This is sufficient to give you the proteins and nutrients you need.

Fill the other quarter of your plate with whole-grain products and starchy foods.

Fill the remaining half of your plate with vegetables of different kinds (raw vegetables, salads, steamed vegetables, etc.) or serve a vegetable soup.

Let your hunger be your guide when choosing the portion to put on your plate. Try to eat a little of everything, but do not force yourself to finish if you are no longer hungry. If you don't have much of an appetite, you should be particularly careful to eat a variety of foods each day, choosing from the three groups (protein, grain products and starchy foods, and vegetables) at each meal.

End your meal with a nutritious dessert, unless you decide to have a nutritious snack later in the daytime or evening.

- Reduce your portions. The size of "normal" portions has nearly doubled in the past 10 years. A restaurant serving, for example, can contain up to 75 percent of the calories you need in an entire day. To help lower your calorie intake, serve yourself smaller portions on a smaller plate, eat slowly, and then serve yourself more if necessary.

- Listen to your body and respect your hunger and satiety signals. Don't eat when you aren't hungry and stop eating when you feel satisfied, even if there is still food on your plate.

- Beware of "light" food products that provide a false sense of security and often lead to an overconsumption of calories. These foods usually contain artificial sweeteners and other food additives that are not healthy.

- Avoid snacking while watching television.

2 REDUCE YOUR OVERALL FAT INTAKE

It is recommended that you reduce your overall fat intake in your diet to help control your blood cholesterol levels. Many foods, including meat and dairy products, already contain significant amounts of fat. One must therefore be conscious of other sources of superfluous fat, such as butter on toast or oil for cooking and seasoning.

When you buy food products, it is important to check the nutritional label and choose products that are not only low in total fat, but also low in saturated and trans fats.

Here is what you should look at on nutritional labels when choosing a food product at the grocery store.

Nutrition Facts
per ½ cup (125 ml)

Amount	% Daily Value
Calories 80	
Fat 0.5 g	1%
Saturated 0 g	
+ Trans 0 g	
Cholesterol 0 mg	
Sodium 0 mg	0%
Carbohydrates 18 g	6%
Fiber 2 g	8%
Sugar 2 g	
Protein 3 g	

Vitamin A	2%	Vitamin C	10%
Calcium	0%	Iron	2%

FAT (in g): Indicates the total amount of fat contained in the serving mentioned. This includes good fat as well as fat that is not so good. Look for foods containing less than 10 percent of the daily recommended value per serving.

SATURATED (in g): Indicates the amount of saturated fat (bad fat) contained in the serving mentioned. Look for foods containing less than 5 percent of the daily recommended value in saturated fat and trans fat per serving.

TRANS (in g): Indicates the amount of trans fat (bad fat) contained in the serving mentioned. Trans fats are strictly to be avoided. Look for foods that do not contain any trans fats.

CHOLESTEROL (in mg): Indicates the amount of cholesterol contained in the serving mentioned. Look for foods that do not contain cholesterol or that contain less than 50 mg of cholesterol per serving.

TIPS FOR REDUCING FAT IN YOUR DIET

- Limit the number of meals you eat at restaurants. When eating out, order grilled meat without sauce, or ask for the sauce on the side. If ordering a salad, ask for the dressing on the side as well.

- Reduce your consumption of processed foods.

- Avoid cream-based soups, dishes topped with cheese or served with white sauce (such as Alfredo sauce), fried foods and breaded foods.

- Avoid muffins, croissants and certain kinds of crackers, and replace cookies and dessert cakes with fruit or low-fat dairy products.

- Choose cheese with 20% m.f. or less, milk and yogurt with 2% m.f. or less, and frozen yogurt or ice milk instead of ice cream. All of these dairy products should be eaten in moderation.

- Replace french fries with baked potatoes, rice or vegetables.

- Limit the amount of butter or margarine you put on your bread.

- Use milk instead of cream in your recipes.

- Reduce the amount of fat called for in dessert recipes by half. Replace the fat with the same amount of unsweetened fruit compote.

- Replace butter with oil or margarine that is high in unsaturated fat (⅔ cup/160 ml oil replaces about 1 cup/250 ml butter).

- Remove fat from meat with a knife before cooking it.

- When cooking, use a nonstick skillet, replace butter with oil (a small quantity) and deglaze your cooking juices before eating. You can defat meat stock by placing it in the refrigerator. The fat will congeal on the surface and can easily be skimmed off.

- Liven up your salads with walnuts, hazelnuts or seeds instead of bacon bits.

- If you feel like snacking, avoid potato chips and choose homemade popcorn, walnuts, pistachio nuts, peanuts, almonds, fresh fruits or homemade muffins.

3 CHOOSE GOOD FATS

MONOUNSATURATED AND POLYUNSATURATED FATS

Monounsaturated fats help to lower "bad" cholesterol (LDL) and have a tendency to maintain and even slightly raise "good" cholesterol (HDL).

> Some sources of good fat:
>
> - **Oils:** canola oil, extra virgin olive oil, hazelnut oil
> - **Nuts and seeds:** almonds, hazelnuts, pecans, pistachio nuts, peanuts, cashew nuts, macadamia nuts, Brazil nuts

Just because unsaturated fats are good fats does not mean you can eat as much as you like. Oils, nuts and seeds are high in calories. Eat them in moderation.

OMEGA-3 FATS

Omega-3 fats are good fats to add to your diet. They are reputed to have a beneficial effect on the cardiovascular system and the brain, and they also play a positive role in lipid profiles. Omega-3 lowers cholesterol and the risk of cardiovascular disease and also reduces inflammation in the arteries.

> Some foods rich in omega-3:
>
> - **Oily fish:** salmon, tuna, herring, mackerel, sardines, shrimp, oysters
> - Chia seeds, ground flax seeds, pumpkin seeds, hemp seeds
> - Walnuts
> - Canola oil and flaxseed oil

If you have cholesterol or cardiovascular problems, it is recommended that you consume 2000 to 4000 mg of omega-3 per day. Even if you eat oily fish two or three times a week, you are not getting enough omega-3. Omega-3 supplements may be helpful. Ask your doctor, pharmacist or dietitian for advice on this subject.

PHYTOSTEROLS

Phytosterols, also called plant sterols, are fats of plant origin. Their structure is similar to that of cholesterol. It is now recognized that the consumption of phytosterols in a diet reduces the absorption of cholesterol in the intestine and helps cholesterol be eliminated in the stool. People with cholesterol problems are advised to consume up to 2 g of phytosterol per day to help improve their lipid profile.

All plants contain phytosterols in varying quantities. The following is a list of the best sources.

FOOD	PORTION	AMOUNT OF PHYTOSTEROL (in mg)
Sesame seeds, dried	¼ cup (60 ml)	264
Corn oil	1 tbsp	136
Peanuts	¼ cup (60 ml)	81
Avocado	½ fruit	78
Sunflower seeds	¼ cup (60 ml)	59
Cashew nuts, dry roasted	¼ cup (60 ml)	52
Red kidney beans, cooked	¾ cup (180 ml)	51
Almonds, unblanched, roasted in oil	¼ cup (60 ml)	47
Olive oil	1 tbsp	31
Lentils	¾ cup (180 ml)	31
Asparagus	6 spears	23
Walnuts	¼ cup (60 ml)	22
Curly lettuce	1 cup (250 ml)	22

You can also find products on the market that are enriched in phytosterols, which include yogurt, orange juice, cheese and soy milk. Margarine and other products labeled "enriched with phytosterols" (as well as those said to be enriched with omega-3), are not always good. Just because they contain a substance said to lower cholesterol does not mean they don't contain saturated fats.

4 REDUCE BAD FATS

TRANS FATS: TO AVOID

They have a doubly harmful effect on cardiovascular health. Along with raising LDL or "bad" blood cholesterol levels, trans fats reduce HDL or "good" blood cholesterol levels. These fats are mainly found in commercially prepared products, from baked goods (cookies, pastries, muffins, cereal bars, crackers, pie dough and pancake mix) to ready-made sauces, fried foods from fast-food establishments and partially hydrogenated margarines.

TIPS FOR AVOIDING TRANS FATS

- Always check nutritional labels before buying a product. If "0" is not indicated next to "trans fats," choose another product.

- Use olive oil or margarine for cooking, or to replace lard and shortening.

- Make your own cakes, muffins and pastries in large quantities so you can freeze them. This will help you save time and is better than using mixes and ready-made products that may contain trans fats and saturated fats.

- Avoid ordering french fries when eating out. Instead, order a green salad, baked potato or rice.

SATURATED FATS: TO REDUCE

Saturated fats are among the fats that have the most impact on blood cholesterol. They are mainly found in products of animal origin. It is recommended that you reduce your consumption of meat, butter, shortening and processed foods, and replace them with sources of good fat. It is also recommended that you consume no more than two to three servings of red meat per week.

SOURCES OF SATURATED FAT	SUBSTITUTES TO CHOOSE WHENEVER POSSIBLE
Meat, poultry and processed meats with more than 10% fat	Meat with less than 10% fat (visible fat removed), white meat of poultry (no skin), tofu, legumes (dried beans, lentils, peas), fish, seafood
Cheese with more than 20% m.f.	Cheese with less than 20% m.f. (in moderation), rice cheese, soy cheese
Coconut butter, coconut oil, palm oil, palm kernel oil	Extra virgin olive oil, canola oil, hazelnut oil, flaxseed oil
Whole milk, sour cream, cream	Milk with less than 2% m.f., sour cream with less than 2% m.f., soy coffee creamer, soy milk, rice milk, almond milk
Yogurt with more than 2% m.f	Yogurt with less than 2% m.f., soy puddings
Butter, lard, hard margarine hydrogenated vegetable oils	Non-hydrogenated margarine or extra virgin olive oil, canola oil, hazelnut oil
Pie crust, flaky pastry, croissants	Olive oil-based pie crust, whole wheat pita bread

BEWARE OF DIETARY CHOLESTEROL

It is now recognized that the cholesterol found in food is not the main factor in high LDL cholesterol. However, you should still avoid consuming excessive amounts of dietary cholesterol. By reducing the sources of saturated fat in your diet, you will reduce the sources of dietary cholesterol at the same time. The principal sources of saturated fat are foods of animal origin, which also contain dietary cholesterol.

Some foods are high in cholesterol and, even if they are low in saturated fat, they should be eaten in moderation:

- Eggs as a meal (omelets, salads, sandwiches): 4 whole eggs or fewer per week

  You can consume up to 7 eggs per week only if you do not suffer from high cholesterol. The egg content in cakes and muffins is very small per portion, so it does not need to be taken into account.

- Shrimp: 2 servings or less per week

- Beef liver

- Beef heart

- Offal of every kind

5 INCREASE YOUR FIBER CONSUMPTION

There are two types of fiber — soluble and insoluble.

SOLUBLE FIBER: TO HELP CONTROL BLOOD CHOLESTEROL

Soluble fiber is preferred, because it binds with cholesterol in the intestine, reducing the absorption of cholesterol in the blood. Microorganisms in the intestinal flora digest this fiber, producing short-chain free fatty acids that limit the production of cholesterol by the liver. This is why it is important to consume a lot of fiber every day, particularly soluble fiber.

It is recommended that you drink plenty of water as part of high-fiber diet — at least 4 to 6 glasses of water per day.

The best sources of soluble fiber:

- **Grain products:** barley and other barley-based products (barley cereals, cream of barley, barley flour), basmati rice, buckwheat, oat and other oat-based products (oat cereals like Cheerios — original version, oat flour, rolled oats, oat bran bread, oat bran), psyllium (All-Bran Buds, Metamucil, psyllium powder), quinoa, rye bread

- **Fruits:** bananas, blackberries, blueberries, clementines, cranberries, grapefruit, lemons, oranges, passion fruit, pineapple, kiwis, kumquats, limes, mandarin oranges, nectarines, rhubarb, tangerines

- **Vegetables:** asparagus, canned artichoke hearts, cooked carrots, sweet potatoes, zucchini

- **Legumes:** chickpeas, cooked beans (black, red, white), mixed beans

- **Seeds:** chia seeds, ground flax seeds, soy nuts

- **Other source:** soy milk

TIPS FOR EATING MORE SOLUBLE FIBER

- Gradually increase your consumption of soluble fiber by choosing oat-based bread instead of wheat bread.

- Choose oatmeal or oat-based cereal for breakfast.

- Add oat bran to your yogurt. Replace some of the wheat flour in your recipes for muffins, crêpes and cakes with oat bran. Some of the breadcrumbs in recipes can be replaced by oat bran as well.

- Increase your consumption of fruit by including fruit in your snacks.

FIBER TO REPLACE REFINED PRODUCTS

As part of a healthy diet, it is important to consume foods that are high in fiber and to limit your consumption of refined foods (such as regular pasta). You should especially avoid refined (white) grain products that do not contain fiber. These products can lead to weight gain and deregulation of blood cholesterol levels. They include the following foods in particular:

- Sliced white bread, white bread hamburger buns and hot dog buns, regular (white) pasta, white rice, pizza dough, donuts, commercially prepared muffins, waffles and croissants.

- Sweetened breakfast cereals without fiber.

TIPS FOR INCREASING FIBER IN YOUR DIET

- Cook with good basic ingredients, such as vegetables, fruits and whole-grain products.

- Eat at least four servings of vegetables per day.

- Vary your sources of grain products with oats (rolled oats for breakfast), quinoa, barley, whole wheat couscous, bulgur, buckwheat and millet.

- Choose whole wheat pasta or, if you don't like brown pasta, serve a half-and-half mixture of regular and whole wheat pasta.

- Choose long-grain white or brown rice containing at least 2 g of fiber per ½ cup (125 ml) serving.

- Eat a handful of walnuts or almonds every day.

- Add ground flax seeds, chia seeds, wheat bran, oat bran, All-Bran cereal or All-Bran Buds . . . to your yogurt, breakfast cereal and batters for pancakes, cakes and muffins.

6 CHOOSE PLANT PROTEIN

Animal protein is known to contain a lot of saturated fat (bad fat), which raises LDL levels. Red meat is known to increase the risk of certain types of cancer. This is why plant protein is good. High in fiber, good fats and often lower in calories, plant protein is filling and helps you avoid high-calorie snacking between meals. It is also important to vary the sources of plant protein in your diet.

Reduce the amount of protein from animal sources consumed each week (two to three servings maximum). Choose lean cuts of meat. In general, choose fish and plant protein over animal protein.

Principal sources of plant protein:

- **Legumes:** red kidney beans, white beans, black beans, lentils, lima beans, lupini beans, chickpeas

- **Nuts and seeds:** almonds, hazelnuts, Brazil nuts, soybeans, sunflower, flax and chia seeds

- **Soy derivatives:** silken tofu, regular tofu, edamame

7 EAT LESS REFINED SUGAR

Consumption of refined sugar increases the risk of cholesterol problems and causes fluctuation in glycemic levels.

Refined sugars are "empty" calories, which means you are consuming calories without really feeling satisfied. As a result, you eat more, and managing your weight becomes even more difficult.

Foods and ingredients rich in refined sugar to avoid:

- Pastries, cakes, cookies, pies, ice cream and ice pops
- Granulated sugar, honey, maple syrup and agave syrup
- Carbonated beverages, fruit juice and fruit cocktail
- Candy and candy bars

TIPS FOR EATING LESS REFINED SUGAR

- Avoid commercially prepared desserts.

- Learn to read nutritional labels and look at the list of ingredients. Look for products in which sugar (or one its forms such as sucrose, fructose, barley malt or corn syrup) is not one of the first three ingredients on the list. Keep an eye out for names that end in -ose, which are usually hidden sugars.

- Choose tap water or mineral water over juices and carbonated beverages, even if they are labeled "diet" or "no added sugar."

- Prepare your own meals and snacks at home as often as possible, and reduce the amount of sugar called for in recipes by half. You can also use unsweetened applesauce to replace sugar in some recipes.

- Do not add granulated sugar to cereal, coffee or tea. If you do, try using less.

8 MODERATE YOUR SODIUM INTAKE

To prevent or lower high blood pressure, which is recognized as a major risk factor in cardiovascular diseases, it is recommended that you moderate your intake of sodium, which favors water retention.

Reduce your consumption of commercially prepared foods, bouillons, potato chips and vegetable juice. Check the amount of sodium in foods and choose those containing less than 15% of the recommended daily value (% DV) of sodium per serving.

Nutrition Facts
per 4 servings

Amount	% Daily Value
Calories 240	
Fat 2 g	3%
Saturated 0,3 g	
+ Trans 0 g	
Cholesterol 0 mg	
Sodium 90 mg	4%
Carbohydrates 51 g	5%
Fiber 3 g	21%
Sugar 1 g	
Protein 2 g	

Vitamin A	0%	Vitamin C	0%
Calcium	2%	Iron	7%

Avoid adding too much salt when cooking and at the table, along with high-sodium seasonings. Choose herbs to enhance the flavor of your dishes instead.

9 REDUCE YOUR ALCOHOL CONSUMPTION

When consumed in excess, alcoholic beverages increase the level of triglycerides (a type of fat in the blood). On the other hand, moderate alcohol consumption does not have a negative effect on lipid profiles. It is recommended that women have a maximum of one drink per day and men a maximum of two drinks per day.

A serving corresponds to:

- a glass of wine (5 oz/150 ml), 12% alcohol content

- a bottle of beer (12 oz/341 ml), 5% alcohol content

- a glass of spirits (1½ oz/45 ml), 40% alcohol content

Some kinds of alcohol, consumed in moderation, may provide protection against cardiovascular disease. Wine provides additional advantages thanks to the plant components in the grapes that help lower cholesterol. That is why we often hear that wine is good for the heart, because of the plant components in the grapes that help lower cholesterol.

FOODS TO CHOOSE

Grain Products

High in soluble fiber: barley, basmati rice, buckwheat, oat, psyllium, quinoa, rye bread.

Other: long-grain brown rice, millet, whole wheat bread and pasta, whole wheat couscous, whole wheat flour, quinoa.

Fruits and Vegetables

Fruits: bananas, blackberries, blueberries, clementines, cranberries, grapefruit, kiwis, kumquats, lemons, limes, mandarin oranges, nectarines, oranges, passion fruit, pineapple, rhubarb, tangerines.

Vegetables: asparagus, canned artichoke hearts, cooked carrots, sweet potatoes zucchini. Choose several vegetables and fill half your plate with them at each main meal.

Legumes and Seeds

Chia seeds, chickpeas, cooked beans (black, red, white), ground flax seeds, lentils, soybeans, split peas.

Oily Fish

Herring, salmon, sardines, trout, tuna. To be consumed at least twice a week.

Lean Animal Protein and Plant Protein

Chicken, eggs, lean beef, nuts and seeds (soy nuts, almonds, walnuts, sunflower seeds), pork, soy milk, tofu.

Vegetable oils

Canola oil, flaxseed oil, olive oil.

Dishes that are steamed, grilled or cooked en papillote

Homemade desserts made with less sugar

Low-fat dairy products

Cheese (20% m.f. or less), milk (2%), yogurt (2% m.f. or less).

FOODS TO AVOID

Refined Sugar

Sweetened breakfast cereals, cakes, candied fruits, candy, carbonated beverages, chocolate, cookies, donuts, fruit juice and fruit cocktail, granulated sugar, honey, ice cream, jam, maple syrup, pastries, pizza dough, regular (white) pasta, sorbets, white bread.

Animal Fats

Butter, cheeses, cream (35% m.f.), crème fraîche, fatty meats, lard, processed meats.

Highly Salted Foods

Canned soups, marinades, processed meats, snack crackers, vegetable juice.

Foods High in Fat

Breaded foods, cream-based sauces, fried foods, pastries, pies, potato chips.

Alcohol

To be consumed in moderation.

21 DAYS
OF MENUS

The menus in this book have been designed to provide you with all the nutrients and energy you require each day.

The meals and snacks are interchangeable from one day to another. You will also see that the lunchtime meals are often leftovers from the previous evening. You should therefore adjust recipe portions accordingly, doubling the amounts if necessary so that you have leftovers for the next day.

Plan your week with the suggested menus, prepare your grocery list and buy the ingredients you are missing for the recipes you have selected.

If you have any doubts or difficulty balancing your diet while following these menus, it is strongly recommended that you see a dietitian who can adapt the menus and portions to your personal needs.

DAY 1

BREAKFAST ....

¾ cup (180 ml) oat cereal
½ cup (125 ml) milk or plain soy milk
1 banana

Snack
10 almonds
1 pear

LUNCH ....

Salmon and Spinach Salad (p. 96)
served with Tortilla Chips (p. 98)

Snack
1 fruit yogurt

DINNER ....

Bean and Beef Patties (p. 100)
served with rice and mixed vegetables
(zucchini, tomatoes, olives, cauliflower and bell peppers)

Snack
1 Oat and Date Cereal Bar (p. 80)

DAY 2

BREAKFAST . . . .

1 Banana and Peanut Butter Smoothie (p. 70)

Snack
1 Oat and Date Cereal Bar (p. 80)

LUNCH . . . .

Bean and Beef Patties (p. 100)
served with rice and mixed vegetables
(zucchini, tomatoes, olives, cauliflower and bell peppers)

Snack
1 orange

DINNER . . . .

Sweet and Sour Tofu (p. 102)
served with quinoa, bell peppers and broccoli

Snack
½ cup (125 ml) oat cereal
½ cup (125 ml) milk or plain soy milk

DAY 3

BREAKFAST

Invigorating Oatmeal (p. 72)

Snack
½ cup (125 ml) grapes
¼ cup (60 ml) sunflower seeds

LUNCH

Sweet and Sour Tofu (p. 102)
served with quinoa, bell peppers and broccoli

Snack
1 fruit yogurt

DINNER

Breaded Almond Chicken Fingers (p. 104)
served with Tabbouleh (p. 106)

Snack
1 Oat and Date Cereal Bar (p. 80)

DAY 4

BREAKFAST . . . .

1 or 2 slices oat bread
1 tbsp natural nut butter
1 pear

Snack
Pineapple Frozen Yogurt (p. 82)

LUNCH . . . .

Chicken Salad (p. 108)

Snack
½ cup (125 ml) unsweetened applesauce

DINNER . . . .

Rice with Tuna (p. 111)
served with green peas and broccoli

Snack
½ cup (125 ml) oat cereal
½ cup (125 ml) milk or plain soy milk

DAY 5

BREAKFAST

¾ cup (180 ml) cottage cheese (1% m.f.)
½ cup (125 ml) fresh strawberries or your choice of fruit
1 tsp maple syrup
1 slice Kamut (khorasan wheat) or oat bran bread

Snack
Asian-Style Grilled Chickpeas (p. 85)

LUNCH

Rice with Tuna (p. 111)
served with green peas and broccoli

Snack
10 almonds
½ cup (125 ml) grapes

DINNER

Bean and Sausage Stew (p. 114)

Snack
1 fruit yogurt

DAY 6

BREAKFAST

1 or 2 servings Fruit and Almond Bread (p. 74)
1 cup (250 ml) milk or plain soy milk
1 banana

Snack
1 orange

LUNCH

1 Chicken Ciabatta Sandwich (p. 116)
served with a dish of your choice of raw vegetables
(carrots, celery, bell peppers, broccoli, etc.)

Snack
¼ cup (60 ml) hummus
½ to 1 cup (125 to 250 ml) raw vegetables

DINNER

Tomato and Garlic Fettuccine (p. 112)
served with a green salad

Snack
Pineapple Frozen Yogurt (p. 82)

DAY 7

BREAKFAST

1 plain yogurt

½ cup (125 ml) Choco-Coco Granola (p. 76)

½ cup (125 ml) berries (your choice of raspberries, strawberries or blackberries)

> **Snack**
> 10 almonds

LUNCH

Rolled Crêpes with Asparagus (p. 119)

> **Snack**
> 1 pear

DINNER

Spicy Sole with Warm Bell Pepper Salad (p. 120) served with brown rice

> **Snack**
> 1 serving of Fruit and Almond Bread (p. 74)

DAY 8

BREAKFAST . . . .

½ whole-grain bagel
1 oz low-fat cheese
1 tbsp reduced-sugar jam
1 banana

| **Snack** | |
| 1 apple | |

LUNCH . . . .

Spicy Sole with Warm Bell Pepper Salad (p. 120)
served with brown rice

| **Snack** | |
| 1 Oat and Date Cereal Bar (p. 80) | |

DINNER . . . .

Crispy Soba Noodle Salad (p. 122)
served with eggs

| **Snack** | |
| 1 fruit yogurt | |

DAY 9

BREAKFAST

¾ cup (180 ml) oat cereal
½ cup (125 ml) milk or plain soy milk
1 orange

Snack
Pear Crumble (p. 86)

LUNCH

Express Meal Salad (p. 124)

Snack
1 oz (30 g) low-fat cheese
½ cup (125 ml) grapes

DINNER

Shrimp with Tomatoes and Lime (p. 126)
served with rice noodles

Snack
Pineapple Frozen Yogurt (p. 82)

DAY 10

BREAKFAST ....

1 Banana and Peanut Butter Smoothie (p. 70)

Snack
10 almonds
1 apple

LUNCH ....

Shrimp with Tomatoes and Lime (p. 126)
served with rice noodles

Snack
1 fruit yogurt

DINNER ....

1 Beef Submarine Sandwich (p. 128)
served with Vegetable Salad (p. 131)

Snack
Pear Crumble (p. 86)

DAY 11

BREAKFAST

1 or 2 slices rye or oat bread
1 tbsp nut butter

Snack
½ cup (125 ml) Strawberry Mango
Compote (p. 89)

LUNCH

1 Beef Submarine Sandwich (p. 128)
served with Vegetable Salad (p. 131)

Snack
1 fruit yogurt

DINNER

Chicken and Rice Casserole (p. 132)

Snack
Pear Crumble (p. 86)

DAY 12

BREAKFAST ....

1 plain yogurt
½ cup (125 ml) Choco-Coco Granola (p. 76)
½ cup (125 ml) raspberries

Snack
1 Oat and Date Cereal Bar (p. 80)

LUNCH ....

Chicken and Rice Casserole (p. 132)

Snack
¼ cup (60 ml) sunflower seeds
1 apple

DINNER ....

Lemon Salmon (p. 135)
served with sweet potato fries and broccoli

Snack
½ cup (125 ml) Strawberry Mango
Compote (p. 89)

DAY 13

BREAKFAST

1 or 2 Peach and Blueberry Crêpes (p. 78)
1 orange

Snack
1 banana

LUNCH

Lemon Salmon (p. 135)
served with sweet potato fries and broccoli

Snack
1 oz (30 g) low-fat cheese
½ cup (125 ml) grapes

DINNER

Scrambled Tofu with Broccoli (p. 136)
served with Tortilla Chips (p. 98)

Snack
1 Oat and Date Cereal Bar (p. 80)

DAY 14

BREAKFAST ·

¾ cup (180 ml) oat cereal
1 cup (250 ml) milk or plain soy milk
1 banana

Snack 1 Bran and Raisin Muffin (p. 90)	

LUNCH ·

Mushroom Omelet (p. 138)
served with 2 slices of toasted whole-grain bread

Snack ½ cup (125 ml) Strawberry Mango Compote (p. 89)	

DINNER ·

1 Veggie Burger (p. 140)
served with a green salad

Snack 1 fruit yogurt	

DAY 15

BREAKFAST

¾ cup (180 ml) cottage cheese

½ cup (125 ml) fresh fruit (your choice of banana, strawberries or raspberries)

1 slice of Kamut (khorasan wheat) or oat bran bread

Snack
1 Healthy Biscotto (p. 93)

LUNCH

1 Veggie Burger (p. 140) served with a green salad

Snack
1 orange

DINNER

Beef Noodle Soup (p. 142)

Snack
1 fruit yogurt

DAY 16

BREAKFAST

1 or 2 servings Fruit and Almond Bread (p. 74)
1 cup (250 ml) milk or plain soy milk
1 banana

Snack
1 fruit yogurt

LUNCH

Beef Noodle Soup (p. 142)

Snack
10 almonds
1 apple

DINNER

Mediterranean Quiche (p. 144)
served with a green salad

Snack
1 Healthy Biscotto (p. 93)

DAY 17

BREAKFAST

1 or 2 slices rye or oat bread
1 tbsp natural nut butter
1 banana

Snack
1 orange

LUNCH

1 Tuna Sandwich (p. 147)
served with raw vegetables

Snack
½ cup (125 ml) unsweetened applesauce

DINNER

Red Kidney Bean Croquettes (p. 148)
served with Tabbouleh (p. 106)

Snack
1 Carrot Cookie (p. 94)
1 cup (250 ml) milk or plain soy milk

DAY 18

BREAKFAST

¾ cup (180 ml) oat cereal
½ cup (125 ml) milk or plain soy milk
½ cup (125 ml) blueberries

Snack
1 Bran and Raisin Muffin (p. 90)

LUNCH

Red Kidney Bean Croquettes (p. 148)
served with Tabbouleh (p. 106)

Snack
½ cup (125 ml) Strawberry Mango
Compote (p. 89)

DINNER

Barley and Chicken Pilaf (p. 150)

Snack
1 fruit yogurt

DAY 19

BREAKFAST ·

Invigorating Oatmeal (p. 72)

Snack
1 apple

LUNCH ·

Barley and Chicken Pilaf (p. 150)

Snack
1 Carrot Cookie (p. 94)

DINNER ·

Avocado and Shrimp Salad (p. 152)

Snack
1 cup (250 ml) milk or plain soy milk

DAY 20

BREAKFAST ....

1 plain yogurt
¼ cup (60 ml) Choco-Coco Granola (p. 76)
½ cup (125 ml) raspberries

Snack
1 Bran and Raisin Muffin (p. 90)

LUNCH ....

1 Bagel with Smoked Salmon (p. 154)
served with raw vegetables

Snack
Pineapple Frozen Yogurt (p. 82)

DINNER ....

Grilled Steak Fajitas (p. 156)
served with Vegetable Salad (p. 131)

Snack
½ cup (125 ml) unsweetened applesauce

DAY 21

BREAKFAST

1 Banana and Peanut Butter Smoothie (p. 70)

Snack
1 peach
¼ cup (60 ml) soy nuts

LUNCH

1 or 2 Peach and Blueberry Crêpes (p. 78)

Snack
Pear Crumble (p. 86)

DINNER

1 Grilled Cheese Sandwich with Apple and Chicken (p. 158) served with Vegetable Salad (p. 131)

Snack
1 Carrot Cookie (p. 94)
1 cup (250 ml) milk or plain soy milk

RECIPES
45 HEALTHY IDEAS

Throughout this chapter, you will find CHOLESTEROL INFO boxes on many healthy foods and how they help to lower cholesterol levels.

BANANA AND PEANUT BUTTER
Smoothie

1 smoothie • PREPARATION: 5 minutes

INGREDIENTS

1 tbsp creamy peanut butter

½ cup (125 ml) plain yogurt

1 very ripe banana

1 tbsp oat bran

½ cup (125 ml) milk
or plain soy milk

1 tsp maple syrup or honey

METHOD

In a microwave-safe dish, melt peanut butter in the microwave for 30 seconds.

In a food processor, combine all ingredients and blend thoroughly.

• • • • • • • • • • • • •

VARIATION

Use other varieties of fruit instead of banana or make a green smoothie by using baby spinach leaves.

CHOLESTEROL INFO

• •

The banana is a fruit that is high in soluble fiber and contains a lot of natural sugar — perfect for satisfying a sweet tooth.

Nutrition Facts Per smoothie	
Amount	
Calories	376
Fat	12 g
Sodium	150 mg
Carbohydrates	56 g
Fiber	5 g
Protein	17 g

INVIGORATING
Oatmeal

1 serving • PREPARATION: 5 minutes • COOKING TIME: 2 minutes

INGREDIENTS

¾ cup (180 ml) milk or soy milk

½ cup (125 ml) quick-cooking rolled oats

1 tsp honey

½ cup (125 ml) fresh raspberries

1 tbsp chia seeds

METHOD

In a microwave-safe bowl, mix together milk and rolled oats. Cook in microwave for 1 minute, stir, then cook for an additional 30 seconds to 1 minute if needed.

Add honey, raspberries and chia seeds. Mix together thoroughly.

• • • • • • • • • • • • •

TIP

Buy quick-cooking (5 minutes) rolled oats in bulk. The faster cooking (one-minute) rolled oats are less nutritious and often more expensive.

CHOLESTEROL INFO

• •

Rolled oats are a good source of energy and soluble fiber. They are a perfect choice for helping you control your appetite and lower your cholesterol.

Nutrition Facts	
Per serving	
Amount	
Calories	240
Fat	7 g
Sodium	90 mg
Carbohydrates	35 g
Fiber	10 g
Protein	11 g

FRUIT AND ALMOND
Bread

24 servings • PREPARATION: 20 minutes • COOKING TIME: 45 minutes

INGREDIENTS

2 cups (500 ml) unbleached all-purpose flour

½ cup (125 ml) oat bran

1 tbsp baking powder

1 tsp baking soda

1 cup (250 ml) chopped almonds

1 cup (250 ml) pumpkin or sunflower seeds

1 cup (250 ml) dried dates, chopped

¼ cup (60 ml) dried cranberries

¼ cup (60 ml) dried apricots, chopped

3 eggs

1 tsp vanilla extract

½ cup (125 ml) unsweetened applesauce

3 tbsp canola oil

METHOD

Position rack in middle of oven and preheat to 350°F (180°C). Grease a 9-inch (23 cm) loaf pan.

In a bowl, mix together flour, oat bran, baking powder, baking soda, almonds, seeds and dried fruits.

In a separate bowl, using an electric beater, beat eggs, vanilla extract, applesauce and canola oil for 1 minute.

Add liquid mixture to dry ingredients and blend thoroughly. Pour into prepared pan. Bake in center of preheated oven for 45 minutes.

Let cool. Cut into 12 slices, then cut each slice in half.

CHOLESTEROL INFO

• •

Using unsweetened applesauce is a good way to lower the amount of fat and sugar in desserts while making them more nutritious.

Nutrition Facts Per serving	
Amount	
Calories	180
Fat	9 g
Sodium	22 mg
Carbohydrates	20 g
Fiber	3 g
Protein	6 g

CHOCO-COCO
Granola

20 servings • PREPARATION: 10 minutes • COOKING TIME: 30 minutes

INGREDIENTS

1 cup (250 ml) unsweetened shredded coconut

2 tbsp canola oil

½ cup (125 ml) maple syrup

1 tbsp vanilla extract

4 cups (1 liter) old-fashioned rolled oats

½ cup (125 ml) unsweetened cocoa powder

1 cup (250 ml) dried cranberries

METHOD

Position rack in middle of oven and preheat to 350°F (180°C). Line a baking sheet with parchment paper.

In a skillet over medium heat, toast shredded coconut, stirring often, for 2 to 3 minutes.

In a bowl, mix together canola oil, maple syrup and vanilla extract. Add coconut, rolled oats and cocoa powder.

Spread granola over entire prepared baking sheet. Bake in center of preheated oven, stirring every 5 minutes, for 25 to 30 minutes, until thoroughly toasted. When granola is ready, add dried cranberries. Let sit before serving.

• • • • • • • • • • • • •

TIP

The mixture keeps in an airtight container for up to 2 weeks at room temperature or several weeks in the refrigerator.

Nutrition Facts	
Per serving	
Amount	
Calories	120
Fat	6 g
Sodium	4 mg
Carbohydrates	20 g
Fiber	3 g
Protein	2 g

PEACH AND BLUEBERRY
Crêpes

4 servings • PREPARATION: 15 minutes • COOKING TIME: 40 minutes

INGREDIENTS

3 peaches, peeled and cut in pieces

1 cup (250 ml) fresh or frozen blueberries

2 tbsp chopped fresh mint

2 tbsp maple syrup

2 cups (500 ml) unbleached all-purpose flour

¼ cup (60 ml) oat bran

4 eggs

1½ cups (375 ml) milk or plain soy milk

Zest of 1 lemon

1 tsp vanilla extract

2 cups (500 ml) cottage cheese (1% m.f.)

METHOD

In a saucepan over medium heat, cook peaches, blueberries, mint and maple syrup for about 15 minutes, until a thick compote is obtained.

Meanwhile, in a bowl, mix together flour, oat bran, eggs, milk, lemon zest and vanilla extract.

In a lightly oiled skillet over medium heat, pour ½ cup (125 ml) of batter at a time. Cook crêpe for 2 to 3 minutes on each side. Repeat procedure until there is no more batter (yields about 8 thin crêpes).

Fill crêpes with ¼ cup (60 ml) cottage cheese and top with fruit compote.

• • • • • • • • • • • • • •

TIP

Always keep some fruit in the freezer for preparing muffins, smoothies, yogurt toppings, etc.

Nutrition Facts
Per serving

Amount	
Calories	550
Fat	9 g
Sodium	600 mg
Carbohydrates	80 g
Fiber	6 g
Protein	22 g

OAT AND DATE
Cereal Bars

16 bars • PREPARATION: 20 minutes • COOKING TIME: 6 minutes • REFRIGERATION: 1 hour

INGREDIENTS

4 cups (1 liter) pitted whole dried dates

1 cup (250 ml) water

3 cups (750 ml) old-fashioned rolled oats

¼ cup (60 ml) unsweetened cocoa powder

1 cup (250 ml) slivered almonds

METHOD

Chop dates and place in a large microwave-safe bowl. Add water. Cook in microwave, stirring once every minute, for 6 minutes, until dates are cooked.

Using a fork, break up dates. Add rolled oats, cocoa powder and slivered almonds.

Line a 9-inch (23 cm) baking dish with parchment paper. Transfer mixture and press down firmly.

Refrigerate for 1 hour. Cut into bars and wrap individually.

CHOLESTEROL INFO

• •

Fresh or dried dates are a good source of fiber and are high in simple carbohydrates, packing a lot of energy. They are also rich in antioxidants.

Nutrition Facts
Per cereal bar

Amount	
Calories	160
Fat	6 g
Sodium	1 mg
Carbohydrates	26 g
Fiber	4 g
Protein	4 g

PINEAPPLE
Frozen Yogurt

4 servings • PREPARATION: 5 minutes

INGREDIENTS

1 cup (250 ml) Greek or regular vanilla yogurt (2% m.f.)

1½ cups (375 ml) frozen pineapple chunks

¼ cup (60 ml) honey

METHOD

In a food processor, blend yogurt, frozen pineapple chunks and honey thoroughly.

Serve immediately or store in the freezer.

• • • • • • • • • • • • •

VARIATION

Replace pineapple with mango or your choice of other frozen fruit for more variety.

TIPS

• Greek yogurt yields much creamier frozen yogurt than ordinary yogurt.

• Remove frozen yogurt from the freezer 10 to 15 minutes before serving.

Nutrition Facts	
Per serving	
Amount	
Calories	160
Fat	2 g
Sodium	35 mg
Carbohydrates	37 g
Fiber	1 g
Protein	3 g

ASIAN-STYLE GRILLED
Chickpeas

6 servings • PREPARATION: 5 minutes • COOKING TIME: 35 minutes

METHOD

Position rack in middle of oven and preheat to 350°F (180°C). Line a baking sheet with parchment paper.

Dry chickpeas with a clean cloth.

In a bowl, mix together chickpeas, sesame oil and seasonings. Transfer seasoned chickpeas to prepared baking sheet. Bake in center of oven for 20 minutes.

Turn chickpeas over with a spatula and continue baking for 15 minutes.

• • • • • • • • • • • • • •

TIP

This recipe keeps a few days at room temperature. It's ideal for garnishing salads and makes a filling snack.

INGREDIENTS

1 can (19 oz/540 ml) chickpeas, drained and rinsed

2 tbsp sesame oil

For the seasoning

1 tbsp garlic powder

1 tsp ground turmeric

¼ tsp curry powder

¼ tsp ground ginger

Salt and black pepper to taste

CHOLESTEROL INFO

• •

Chickpeas are a good source of plant protein and contain soluble fiber. They help control blood cholesterol levels.

Nutrition Facts Per serving	
Amount	
Calories	140
Fat	6 g
Sodium	4 mg
Carbohydrates	17 g
Fiber	3 g
Protein	6 g

PEAR
Crumble

9 servings • PREPARATION: 15 minutes • COOKING TIME: 20 minutes

INGREDIENTS

6 ripe Bartlett pears, diced

¼ cup (60 ml) brown sugar

2 cups (500 ml) old-fashioned rolled oats

1 cup (125 ml) quick-cooking rolled oats

2 tbsp maple syrup

¼ cup (60 ml) non-hydrogenated margarine, melted

METHOD

Position rack in middle of oven and preheat to 350°F (180°C).

Spread pears in a 9-inch (23 cm) square baking dish. Sprinkle with brown sugar.

In a bowl, mix together rolled oats, maple syrup and margarine.

Spread mixture on top of pears. Bake in center of oven for 20 minutes.

• • • • • • • • • • • • •

TIP

This recipe freezes well.

CHOLESTEROL INFO

Canola and olive oil are perfect for replacing butter in recipes, because they contain less saturated fat than butter. For dessert recipes (cakes, muffins, etc.), non-hydrogenated margarine can be used to replace the same quantity of butter.

Nutrition Facts	
Per serving	
Amount	
Calories	237
Fat	7 g
Sodium	50 mg
Carbohydrates	40 g
Fiber	6 g
Protein	5 g

STRAWBERRY MANGO
Compote

8 servings • PREPARATION: 15 minutes • COOKING TIME: 8 minutes

METHOD

In a large microwave-safe bowl, cook fruit in the microwave for 8 minutes in 2-minute stages. Open oven door at each stage to prevent mixture from boiling over.

Let sit for 5 minutes. Transfer mixture to a food processor and purée until smooth. Let cool before serving.

• • • • • • • • • • • • •

VARIATION

Prepare homemade compotes with a variety of fruits, using apples, pears, raspberries, peaches, etc.

TIPS

- Fruits naturally contain sugar and do not need to have sugar added to them when preparing a compote.

- This compote keeps up to 7 days in the refrigerator and can be used to sweeten muffin recipes, desserts and yogurts.

INGREDIENTS

4 cups (1 liter) chopped strawberries

4 cups (1 liter) chopped fresh mango

Nutrition Facts	
Per serving	
Amount	
Calories	96
Fat	0 g
Sodium	3 mg
Carbohydrates	24 g
Fiber	4 g
Protein	1 g

BRAN AND RAISIN
Muffins

12 muffins • PREPARATION: 15 minutes • COOKING TIME: 25 minutes

INGREDIENTS

1 cup (250 ml) whole wheat flour
1 cup (250 ml) quick-cooking rolled oats
¼ cup (60 ml) oat bran
1 tbsp baking powder
1 tbsp canola oil
¼ cup (60 ml) molasses or maple syrup
2 eggs
¾ cup (180 ml) milk
1½ cups (375 ml) raisins

METHOD

Position rack in middle of oven and pre-heat to 350°F (180°C).

In a large bowl, mix together flour, rolled oats, oat bran and baking powder.

In a separate bowl, beat canola oil, molasses or maple syrup and eggs for 2 minutes. Add milk gradually while beating.

Pour wet ingredients into bowl of dry ingredients and mix together thoroughly. Then add raisins.

Pour mixture into a lightly greased muffin pan. Bake in center of oven for 20 to 25 minutes or until a toothpick inserted in middle of muffin comes out clean.

• • • • • • • • • • • • •

TIP

When preparing muffins, make more than you need. You can freeze some in order to have nutritious and filling snacks on hand at any time.

Nutrition Facts	
Per muffin	
Amount	
Calories	195
Fat	6 g
Sodium	50 mg
Carbohydrates	30 g
Fiber	3 g
Protein	4 g

CHOLESTEROL INFO

• •

Oat bran is a good way to add soluble fiber to muffins, cakes and desserts. It helps control hunger as well as blood cholesterol and sugar levels. Oats are an essential ingredient and can be incorporated in desserts, breakfasts, crêpes and main meals.

Biscotti

12 biscotti • PREPARATION: 15 minutes • COOKING TIME: 45 minutes • RESTING TIME: 20 minutes

METHOD

Position rack in middle of oven and preheat to 350°F (180°C). Line a baking sheet with parchment paper.

In a bowl, mix together flour, rolled oats and baking powder.

In a separate bowl, using an electric beater, beat egg and sugar for 1 minute. Add milk, margarine, vanilla extract and orange zest. Beat for a few seconds until thoroughly blended.

Gradually add dry mixture to wet mixture, beating at low speed. Add almonds and cranberries one spoonful at a time.

Form dough into an 8 x 2 inch (20 x 5 cm) log, about 1 inch (2.5 cm) thick. Place log on prepared baking sheet.

Bake in center of oven for 25 minutes.

Remove from oven and let cool for 20 minutes. Using a knife, cut log diagonally into slices about ½ inch (1 cm) thick to form 12 biscotti.

Reduce oven temperature to 300°F (150°C). Place biscotti on same baking sheet and return to oven for 15 to 20 minutes. Remove from oven and let cool on a rack.

• • • • • • • • • • • • •

TIP

These biscotti can be served as a dessert or snack to replace commercially prepared cookies, which are often high in sugar and fat.

INGREDIENTS

1 cup (250 ml) unbleached all-purpose flour

¾ cup (180 ml) quick-cooking rolled oats

1 tsp baking powder

1 egg

½ cup (125 ml) granulated sugar

½ cup (60 ml) milk

¼ cup (60 ml) non-hydrogenated margarine

1 tsp vanilla extract

Zest of 1 orange

½ cup (125 ml) slivered almonds

½ cup (125 ml) dried cranberries

Nutrition Facts Per biscotto	
Amount	
Calories	150
Fat	8 g
Sodium	40 mg
Carbohydrates	16 g
Fiber	2 g
Protein	4 g

CARROT
Cookies

18 cookies • PREPARATION: 15 minutes • COOKING TIME: 15 minutes

INGREDIENTS

1 can (19 oz/540 ml) white beans, drained and rinsed

2 tbsp water

1 cup (250 ml) unbleached all-purpose flour

½ cup (125 ml) old-fashioned rolled oats

¼ cup (60 ml) unsweetened coconut flakes

1½ tsp baking powder

2 eggs

3 tbsp canola oil

½ cup (125 ml) brown sugar

1½ cups (375 ml) grated carrot

½ cup (125 ml) raisins

1 tsp cinnamon powder

METHOD

Position rack in middle of oven and preheat to 350°F (180°C). Line a baking sheet with parchment paper.

In a food processor, blend beans with water into a purée. Add remaining ingredients and blend for 15 to 30 seconds to form a dough.

Using an ice cream spoon, form circles of about 2 inches (5 cm) in diameter and place on prepared baking sheet, leaving space between each cookie. Bake in center of oven for 15 minutes.

CHOLESTEROL INFO

White beans can easily be added to a variety of dessert recipes. They are low in fat and add a soft texture. As well, they are high in soluble fiber and help control blood cholesterol levels.

Nutrition Facts	
Per cookie	
Amount	
Calories	135
Fat	4 g
Sodium	15 mg
Carbohydrates	22 g
Fiber	2 g
Protein	4 g

SALMON AND SPINACH
Salad

4 servings • PREPARATION: 15 minutes • COOKING TIME: 6 minutes

INGREDIENTS

1 large (14 oz/390 g) uncooked salmon fillet, diced

2 tbsp olive oil, divided

6 cups (1.5 liters) baby spinach leaves

2 yellow bell peppers, finely diced

½ cup (125 ml) cashew nuts

1 cup (250 ml) fresh grapes, cut in half

Juice of 1 lemon

For the seasoning

1 tsp dried thyme

1 tsp dried basil

Salt and black pepper

METHOD

In a skillet over high heat, sauté salmon cubes and seasonings in 1 tbsp of the olive oil. Cook for 5 to 6 minutes or until salmon is cooked through.

In a bowl, mix together spinach, bell peppers, cashew nuts and grapes. Add salmon and sprinkle with remaining olive oil and lemon juice.

Serve with Tortilla Chips (p. 98).

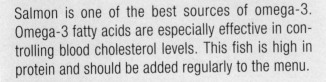

CHOLESTEROL INFO

Salmon is one of the best sources of omega-3. Omega-3 fatty acids are especially effective in controlling blood cholesterol levels. This fish is high in protein and should be added regularly to the menu.

Nutrition Facts	
Per serving	
Amount	
Calories	360
Fat	20 g
Sodium	85 mg
Carbohydrates	20 g
Fiber	3 g
Protein	25 g

TORTILLA
Chips

6 servings • PREPARATION: 10 minutes • COOKING TIME: 5 minutes

INGREDIENTS

3 large whole wheat tortillas

1 tbsp olive oil

For the seasoning

1 tbsp paprika

1 tbsp dried oregano

Salt and black pepper

METHOD

Position rack in middle of oven and pre-heat to 350°F (180°C).

In a small bowl, combine paprika, oregano, salt and black pepper.

Cut tortillas into wedges. Using a basting brush, brush both sides of tortilla wedges with olive oil. Sprinkle seasonings on top. Place on baking sheet and bake in center of oven for about 5 minutes.

• • • • • • • • • • • • • •

TIPS

• Tortilla Chips keep at room temperature for up to 5 days. Note that they are a lot less oily than store-bought crackers or potato chips.

• Keep tortillas in the freezer to always have some on hand.

Nutrition Facts	
Per serving	
Amount	
Calories	176
Fat	6 g
Sodium	230 mg
Carbohydrates	26 g
Fiber	2 g
Protein	4 g

BEAN AND BEEF
Patties

5 servings • PREPARATION: 20 minutes • COOKING TIME: 20 minutes

INGREDIENTS

1 cup (250 ml) long-grain brown rice

1 tbsp low-sodium chicken bouillon powder

8 oz (225 g) lean ground beef

½ cup (125 ml) canned black beans, drained and rinsed

½ cup (125 ml) breadcrumbs

1 onion, minced

1 garlic clove, crushed

1 tbsp olive oil

2 zucchini, diced

10 oz (284 ml) canned diced tomatoes

½ cup (125 ml) black olives, cut in pieces

2 cups (500 ml) cauliflower florets

2 red bell peppers, cut in pieces

For the seasoning

1 tsp dried thyme

1 tsp paprika

Salt and black pepper

METHOD

Cook rice according to directions on package with chicken bouillon.

In food processor, blend ground beef, black beans, breadcrumbs and seasonings. Using your hands, form mixture into 5 patties.

In a heated skillet over medium heat, gently fry onion and garlic in olive oil. Add patties and cook for 5 minutes, turning over once or twice during cooking.

Add vegetables and continue cooking for 5 to 6 minutes.

Serve patties and vegetables with rice.

Nutrition Facts	
Per serving	
Amount	
Calories	380
Fat	10 g
Sodium	540 mg
Carbohydrates	53 g
Fiber	6 g
Protein	18 g

SWEET AND SOUR
Tofu

4 servings • PREPARATION: 15 minutes • COOKING TIME: 20 minutes

INGREDIENTS

¾ cup (180 ml) uncooked quinoa, rinsed

2 cups (500 ml) water, divided

3 tbsp rice vinegar

3 tbsp ketchup

1 tbsp cornstarch

¼ cup (60 ml) granulated sugar

1 tbsp low-sodium soy sauce

1 lb (454 g) tofu, cut into cubes and blotted dry

2 tbsp sesame oil

2 red bell peppers, cut in strips

2 cups (500 ml) broccoli florets

METHOD

In a saucepan over medium-high heat, cook quinoa in 1½ cups (375 ml) water for about 10 minutes until there is no water left in saucepan.

In a bowl, mix together rice vinegar, ketchup, cornstarch, sugar, soy sauce and ½ cup (125 ml) water. Set aside.

In a large skillet over high heat, sauté tofu for 5 minutes in sesame oil.

Reduce heat to medium-low. Add bell peppers and broccoli. Fry gently for 2 minutes. Remove skillet from heat and add sauce. Mix thoroughly and serve on a bed of quinoa.

• • • • • • • • • • • • • •

TIP

Tofu needs to be cooked with a sauce and seasonings or thoroughly marinated ahead of time to give it good flavor. You can marinate it the same way as chicken or beef.

CHOLESTEROL INFO

Soy products, including tofu, are rich in plant protein and good fats. These two health partners help control hunger and blood cholesterol levels.

Nutrition Facts Per serving	
Amount	
Calories	380
Fat	14 g
Sodium	300 mg
Carbohydrates	50 g
Fiber	6 g
Protein	14 g

BREADED ALMOND
Chicken Fingers

4 servings • PREPARATION: 25 minutes • COOKING TIME: 15 minutes

INGREDIENTS

14 oz (390 g) boneless, skinless chicken, cut in strips

2 tbsp whole wheat flour

1 egg

2 tbsp water

1 tbsp Dijon mustard

⅓ cup (80 ml) chopped almonds

3 tbsp breadcrumbs

For the seasoning

½ tsp garlic powder

1 tsp dried basil

1 tsp paprika

Salt and black pepper

METHOD

Preheat oven to 375°F (190°C). Line a baking sheet with parchment paper.

Flatten chicken strips with a mallet or saucepan.

Place flour in a bowl.

In a separate bowl, beat egg with water and Dijon mustard.

In a dish, mix together almonds, breadcrumbs and seasonings.

Coat chicken in flour. Dip chicken in beaten egg mixture, then in almond and breadcrumb mixture.

Place chicken strips on prepared baking sheet and bake for 7 minutes. Turn chicken over and continue baking for 8 minutes.

Serve chicken strips with Tabbouleh (p. 106).

• • • • • • • • • • • • •

Nutrition Facts	
Per serving	
Amount	
Calories	376
Fat	12 g
Sodium	150 mg
Carbohydrates	56 g
Fiber	5 g
Protein	17 g

TIP

Making your own breaded chicken fingers is a good way to enjoy this meal while cutting down on the amount of fat consumed for the same dish found in restaurants and frozen products.

8 servings • PREPARATION: 15 minutes • RESTING TIME: 2 hours

INGREDIENTS

2 cups (500 ml) uncooked whole-grain bulgur

3 tbsp olive oil

½ cup (125 ml) chopped fresh parsley

4 large tomatoes, diced

1 green pepper, diced

Juice of 2 lemons

For the seasoning

Salt and black pepper

METHOD

In a bowl, mix together all ingredients and let sit for 2 hours in the refrigerator.

Season to taste.

• • • • • • • • • • • • •

VARIATION

Replace bulgur with the same amount of whole wheat couscous.

TIPS

- Add olive oil or lemon juice if the salad seems too dry.
- This tabbouleh keeps up to 7 days in the refrigerator.

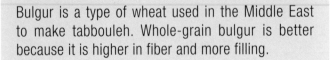

CHOLESTEROL INFO

• •

Bulgur is a type of wheat used in the Middle East to make tabbouleh. Whole-grain bulgur is better because it is higher in fiber and more filling.

Nutrition Facts Per serving	
Amount	
Calories	230
Fat	6 g
Sodium	9 mg
Carbohydrates	38 g
Fiber	3 g
Protein	6 g

CHICKEN
Salad

4 servings • PREPARATION: 15 minutes • COOKING TIME: 10 minutes

INGREDIENTS

14 oz (390 g) boneless, skinless chicken breast, cut in strips

1 tbsp canola oil

3 cups (750 ml) chopped romaine lettuce

1 cup (250 ml) slivered almonds

1 zucchini, diced

2 cups (500 ml) cherry tomatoes

1 cup (250 ml) garlic croutons

3 tbsp extra virgin olive oil

1 tbsp lemon juice

For the seasoning

1 tsp paprika

1 tsp garlic powder

2 tbsp chopped fresh mint

METHOD

In a heated skillet over high heat, sauté chicken in canola oil with paprika and garlic powder. Cook for 1 minute on each side, then reduce heat to medium. Continue cooking for 6 to 7 minutes, until chicken is no longer pink inside.

In a large bowl, mix together lettuce, almonds, zucchini, tomatoes and croutons.

In a bowl, prepare vinaigrette by blending olive oil, lemon juice and fresh mint.

Arrange chicken strips on salad, then drizzle vinaigrette on top.

• • • • • • • • • • • • • •

TIP

Save cooked chicken pieces in the freezer to make it easier to prepare a meal when you are in a hurry.

CHOLESTEROL INFO

• •

Almonds are high in fiber, protein and good fats, which are essential in controlling blood cholesterol levels and maintaining overall health.

Nutrition Facts Per serving	
Amount	
Calories	530
Fat	35 g
Sodium	205 mg
Carbohydrates	22 g
Fiber	4 g
Protein	33 g

4 servings • PREPARATION: 10 minutes • COOKING TIME: 20 minutes

METHOD

Cook rice according to directions on package with chicken bouillon.

In a large skillet over medium heat, gently fry garlic in olive oil for 1 minute.

Add tuna and vegetables. Stir and heat for 4 to 5 minutes.

Mix with cooked rice and serve.

• • • • • • • • • • • • • •

TIPS

• Replace canned green peas with frozen green peas.

• To save time preparing meals, keep cooked brown rice frozen in servings. A half cup (125 ml) uncooked brown rice yields about 2 cups (500 ml) cooked rice. This will help you avoid using "minute" rice, which is less nutritious.

INGREDIENTS

1 cup (250 ml) uncooked brown rice

1 tbsp low-sodium chicken bouillon powder

1 clove garlic, crushed

1 tsp olive oil

2 cans (3 ½ oz/105 g)
or 1 can (7 oz/198 g) tuna, drained

1 cup (250 ml) canned green peas

2 cups (500 ml) broccoli florets

For the seasoning

1 tbsp dried thyme

Salt and black pepper

CHOLESTEROL INFO

• •

Brown rice is better than white rice, because it is high in soluble fiber, which is essential for helping control blood cholesterol levels. It is also filling and excellent for intestinal health.

Nutrition Facts Per serving	
Amount	
Calories	285
Fat	4 g
Sodium	190 mg
Carbohydrates	40 g
Fiber	3 g
Protein	20 g

TOMATO AND GARLIC
Fettuccine

6 servings • PREPARATION: 15 minutes • COOKING TIME: 15 minutes

INGREDIENTS

13 oz (370 g) whole wheat fettuccine noodles

3 tbsp olive oil

½ cup (125 ml) unsalted sunflower seeds

3 cloves garlic, cut in half

2 cups (500 ml) cherry tomatoes

14 oz (400 g) bocconcini cheese, cut in pieces

¼ cup (60 ml) Parmesan cheese

For the seasoning

2 tbsp chopped fresh basil

Salt and black pepper

METHOD

Cook noodles according to directions on package.

Heat oil in a separate saucepan over medium heat. Add sunflower seeds, garlic, salt and black pepper and fry gently for 2 minutes. Remove saucepan from heat and let sit for 2 minutes. Add noodles and mix together thoroughly.

Transfer mixture to a serving bowl and garnish with tomatoes, bocconcini, Parmesan and basil.

Serve with a green salad or Vegetable Salad (p. 131).

Nutrition Facts	
Per serving	
Amount	
Calories	488
Fat	23 g
Sodium	211 mg
Carbohydrates	50 g
Fiber	7 g
Protein	20 g

BEAN AND SAUSAGE
Stew

6 servings • PREPARATION: 15 minutes • COOKING TIME: 55 minutes

INGREDIENTS

4 mild Italian sausages
(about 7 oz/210 g)

2 tbsp unbleached all-purpose flour

1 medium onion, minced

1 tbsp olive oil

1 can (19 oz/540 ml) salt-free diced tomatoes

1 can (19 oz/540 ml) white beans, drained and rinsed

1 can (5 ½ oz/156 ml) tomato paste

4 small potatoes, peeled and cut in large cubes

1 tbsp low-sodium beef bouillon powder

1 cup (250 ml) water

For the seasoning

1 tbsp dried basil

1 tbsp dried thyme

Salt and black pepper

METHOD

Preheat oven to 350°F (180°C).

In a saucepan of water over medium-high heat, boil sausages for 10 minutes. Drain and let cool. (This step can be done ahead of time.)

Cut sausages into 4 or 5 large pieces and coat in flour.

In an ovenproof pot, over high heat, sauté onion in olive oil for 2 minutes, then add sausage pieces and sauté for 1 minute.

Add remaining ingredients and water. Bring to a boil, then place in preheated oven and cook for 40 minutes.

Nutrition Facts	
Per serving	
Amount	
Calories	400
Fat	17 g
Sodium	730 mg
Carbohydrates	47 g
Fiber	9 g
Protein	17 g

CHOLESTEROL INFO

Legumes are a good source of soluble fiber, protein and nutrients. Adding small quantities to a meat dish helps to lower the fat content and raise the nutritional value of a meal.

CHICKEN CIABATTA
Sandwiches

4 sandwiches • PREPARATION: 10 minutes

INGREDIENTS

7 oz (210 g) cooked chicken (approx.), in bite-sized pieces

1 cup (250 ml) chopped celery

2 tbsp plain Greek yogurt

2 tbsp Dijon mustard

4 whole-grain ciabatta rolls, cut in half

2 tomatoes, sliced

4 lettuce leaves

For the seasoning

1 tsp garlic powder

1 tsp dried basil

Salt and black pepper

METHOD

In a bowl, mix together chicken, celery, yogurt, Dijon mustard and seasonings.

Garnish ciabatta rolls with chicken salad, tomatoes and lettuce.

Serve with a dish of your choice of raw vegetables (carrots, cucumber, radishes, cauliflower, broccoli, etc.).

• • • • • • • • • • • • • •

TIP

Carrots, cucumber, radishes, cauliflower and broccoli are excellent raw vegetables to pack in a lunchbox.

Nutrition Facts
Per sandwich

Amount	
Calories	237
Fat	4 g
Sodium	400 mg
Carbohydrates	30 g
Fiber	4 g
Protein	23 g

ROLLED CRÊPES
with Asparagus

4 servings • PREPARATION: 25 minutes • COOKING TIME: 40 minutes

METHOD

Prepare crêpe batter by mixing together flour, bran, eggs and milk. Beat batter thoroughly.

In a lightly oiled skillet over medium heat, pour ½ cup (125 ml) of batter at a time to make 8 very thin crêpes. Cook for 2 to 3 minutes on each side.

Meanwhile, cook fresh asparagus spears in boiling water for 8 to 10 minutes. If asparagus is frozen, place in microwave for 2 to 3 minutes.

On each crêpe, lay 5 asparagus spears and ¼ cup (60 ml) cheese. Roll up crêpes and place in a microwave-safe dish. Reheat crêpes for 1 to 2 minutes in microwave to melt cheese.

Serve 2 crêpes per person.

• • • • • • • • • • • • •

TIP

Crêpes can be prepared ahead to save time and they also freeze well.

INGREDIENTS

1½ cups (375 ml) unbleached all-purpose flour

¼ cup (60 ml) oat bran or wheat bran

3 eggs

2 cups (500 ml) milk

40 fresh, frozen or canned asparagus

2 cups (500 ml) grated Swiss cheese

Nutrition Facts Per serving	
Amount	
Calories	437
Fat	10 g
Sodium	250 mg
Carbohydrates	53 g
Fiber	5 g
Protein	35 g

SPICY SOLE
with Warm Bell Pepper Salad

4 servings • PREPARATION: 20 minutes • COOKING TIME: 25 minutes

INGREDIENTS

1 cup (250 ml) uncooked brown rice

1 tbsp low-sodium chicken bouillon powder

4 sole fillets (14 oz/390 g)

1 tbsp canola oil

1 tbsp olive oil

1 clove garlic, minced

1 red bell pepper, cut in strips

1 green bell pepper, cut in strips

1 yellow bell pepper, cut in strips

1 tsp balsamic vinegar

For the seasoning

1 tbsp paprika

1 tsp Cajun seasoning

1 tsp chili powder

Salt and black pepper

METHOD

Cook rice according to directions on package with chicken bouillon.

In a small bowl, combine seasonings. Coat sole fillets in seasonings. Heat oil in a skillet over medium-high heat, add fillets and cook for about 2 minutes on each side for small fillets and 3 minutes for large fillets.

In another skillet, heat olive oil over medium heat and gently fry garlic. Add bell peppers and balsamic vinegar and cook for 5 minutes.

Serve fillets of sole with brown rice and bell peppers.

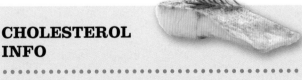

CHOLESTEROL INFO

• •

It is recommended that you eat fish at least twice a week to replace meat. It is scientifically proven that the protein in fish is beneficial to your health.

Nutrition Facts Per serving	
Amount	
Calories	368
Fat	10 g
Sodium	350 mg
Carbohydrates	44 g
Fiber	3 g
Protein	25 g

CRISPY SOBA NOODLE
Salad

4 servings • PREPARATION: 20 minutes • COOKING TIME: 30 minutes

INGREDIENTS

4 oz (115 g) soba noodles

2 tbsp sesame oil

6 cups (1.5 liters) water

1 tbsp white vinegar

8 eggs

¼ cup (60 ml) rice vinegar

2 tbsp granulated sugar

2 to 3 drops Tabasco sauce

2 red bell peppers, chopped

2 carrots, grated

1½ cups (375 ml) chopped pineapple

METHOD

In a saucepan filled with water, on medium-high heat, cook soba noodles for 5 minutes. Drain and blot dry with paper towel.

In a large skillet over medium-high heat, heat sesame oil and add half the soba noodles. Toast noodles for 7 minutes, stirring frequently to make crispy without burning.

In another saucepan, bring water and white vinegar to a low boil. To poach eggs, break eggs one at a time into bubbling water and use a spoon to keep the white around each egg yolk. Cook 4 eggs at a time for 7 minutes, or until white is set but yolk is still runny. Use a slotted spoon to remove eggs, then place on a paper towel.

In a measuring cup, mix together rice vinegar, sugar and Tabasco sauce.

On each plate, place soba noodles and crispy noodles. Garnish with bell peppers, carrots and pineapple. Drizzle with sauce, then place 2 poached eggs on top of each salad.

Nutrition Facts	
Per serving	
Amount	
Calories	475
Fat	17 g
Sodium	600 mg
Carbohydrates	65 g
Fiber	3 g
Protein	20 g

CHOLESTEROL INFO

Eggs are very nutritious and easy to cook. However, they do contain dietary cholesterol. If you have high cholesterol, it is recommended not to consume more than 4 whole eggs per week.

Salad

4 servings • PREPARATION: 15 minutes

INGREDIENTS

3 tbsp olive oil

1 tbsp Dijon mustard

1 clove garlic, crushed

1 tsp granulated sugar

2 tbsp water

2 cans (each 19 oz/540 ml)
mixed beans, drained and rinsed

1 cup (250 ml) green olives

1 cup (250 ml) peeled and
diced cucumber

1 carrot, peeled and diced

1 cup (250 ml) chopped green beans

For the seasoning

1 tsp dried thyme

1 tsp dried oregano

Salt and black pepper

METHOD

In a bowl, mix together oil, Dijon mustard, garlic, sugar, seasonings and water. Blend thoroughly and set aside.

In another bowl, mix together beans, olives and vegetables. Add vinaigrette, mix again, then serve.

Nutrition Facts	
Per serving	
Amount	
Calories	485
Fat	14 g
Sodium	635 mg
Carbohydrates	60 g
Fiber	11 g
Protein	18 g

CHOLESTEROL INFO

Vegetables are high in fiber, which helps control appetite, sugar cravings and blood cholesterol levels. Consume at least two different vegetables at each meal.

SHRIMP
with Tomatoes and Lime

4 servings • PREPARATION: 15 minutes • COOKING TIME: 15 minutes

INGREDIENTS

1 lb 5 oz (600 g) large frozen shrimp

4½ oz (135 g) rice noodles

1 egg

1 cup (250 ml) breadcrumbs

1 tbsp canola oil

1 can (14 oz/398 ml) diced tomatoes

1 green bell pepper, cut in pieces

A few leaves fresh cilantro

Juice of 1 lime

For the seasoning

1 tbsp paprika

1 tsp Cajun seasoning

1 tsp garlic powder

A few drops Tabasco sauce

Salt and black pepper

METHOD

Thaw shrimp according to directions on package, or overnight in refrigerator. Devein if necessary. Blot dry with a clean dishcloth.

Cook rice noodles according to directions on package.

In a bowl, beat egg with a fork.

In another bowl, mix together breadcrumbs and seasonings (except Tabasco sauce).

Dip shrimp in egg, then coat in breadcrumbs.

In a skillet over high heat, sauté shrimp in canola oil for 30 seconds on each side, then reduce heat and cook for 1 minute. Remove shrimp from skillet and set aside.

Add drained rice noodles to skillet, then add tomatoes, bell pepper and Tabasco sauce. Add salt and black pepper to taste. Reheat for about 5 minutes over medium heat.

Serve noodles and tomatoes with shrimp. Garnish with cilantro and sprinkle with lime juice

Nutrition Facts
Per serving

Amount	
Calories	398
Fat	7 g
Sodium	530 mg
Carbohydrates	55 g
Fiber	4 g
Protein	25 g

BEEF SUBMARINE
Sandwiches

4 sandwiches • PREPARATION: 10 minutes • COOKING TIME: 6 minutes

INGREDIENTS

12 oz (340 g) beef for fondue

1 tbsp canola oil

1 red bell pepper, cut in strips

1 yellow bell pepper, cut in strips

4 small whole-grain submarine rolls

A few lettuce leaves

For the seasoning

1 tsp mustard powder

1 tsp garlic powder

A few red pepper flakes

1 tsp ground black pepper

Salt

METHOD

In a skillet over medium-high heat, cook beef in canola oil with strips of bell pepper and seasonings for 5 to 6 minutes.

Fill each submarine roll with beef, strips of bell pepper and lettuce leaves.

Serve sandwiches with a green salad or Vegetable Salad (p. 131).

Nutrition Facts	
Per sandwich	
Amount	
Calories	270
Fat	9 g
Sodium	200 mg
Carbohydrates	26 g
Fiber	3 g
Protein	20 g

VEGETABLE
Salad

4 servings • PREPARATION: 15 minutes

METHOD

In a bowl, mix together all vegetables.

Prepare vinaigrette in a measuring cup, blending olive oil, red wine vinegar, honey and seasonings.

Toss salad with vinaigrette and serve.

. . . .

TIP

Prepare your raw vegetables at the beginning of the week to save time. All you will need to do is toss them with vinaigrette before serving.

INGREDIENTS

3 Italian tomatoes, diced

1 English cucumber, diced

1 yellow bell pepper, diced

2 cups (500 ml) cauliflower florets

3 tbsp olive oil

1 tbsp red wine vinegar

1 tsp honey

For the seasoning

1 tsp dried parsley

1 tsp dried basil

Salt and black pepper

CHOLESTEROL INFO

Olive oil is known for its anti-inflammatory powers as well as its beneficial effect on blood cholesterol levels.

Nutrition Facts Per serving	
Amount	
Calories	140
Fat	10 g
Sodium	20 mg
Carbohydrates	11 g
Fiber	2 g
Protein	2 g

CHICKEN AND RICE
Casserole

5 servings • PREPARATION: 15 minutes • COOKING TIME: 40 minutes

INGREDIENTS

1 cup (250 ml) uncooked brown rice

7 oz (210 g) boneless, skinless chicken breast, diced

1 tbsp canola oil

½ can (14 oz/398 ml) corn

1 can (19 oz/540 ml) black beans, drained and rinsed

1 cup (250 ml) plain Greek yogurt

¾ cup (180 ml) salsa

1 cup (250 ml) shredded low-fat Cheddar cheese, divided

For the seasoning

1 tsp dried basil

1 tbsp dried parsley

Salt and black pepper

METHOD

Position rack in middle of oven and pre-heat to 350°F (180°C).

Cook rice according to directions on package.

In a heated skillet over high heat, cook chicken in canola oil, turning pieces occasionally, for 6 to 8 minutes.

In a large bowl, mix together cooked rice, chicken, corn, beans, yogurt, salsa, half the Cheddar cheese and seasonings.

Place mixture in a 9-inch (23 cm) square baking dish. Top with remaining Cheddar cheese. Bake in center of oven for 15 minutes. Then finish cooking under broiler for a few minutes to brown cheese.

• • • • • • • • • • • • •

TIP

Prepare this recipe more quickly by using 2 cups (500 ml) cooked rice (leftovers or rice that has been frozen in portions).

Nutrition Facts	
Per serving	
Amount	
Calories	450
Fat	10 g
Sodium	482 mg
Carbohydrates	60 g
Fiber	8 g
Protein	30 g

LEMON
Salmon

METHOD

Position rack in middle of oven and preheat to 350°F (180°C).

Rinse sweet potatoes and dry with a clean dishcloth.

In a bowl, coat sweet potatoes in 1 tbsp of the olive oil and 1 tsp of the thyme. Add a pinch of salt and black pepper. Lay sweet potatoes on a baking sheet and bake in preheated oven for 30 to 35 minutes.

Lay salmon fillets on a sheet of aluminum foil. Place slices of lemon, onion, remaining olive oil and thyme on fish. Add salt and pepper. Fold up aluminum foil and bake fish in center of preheated oven for 20 minutes.

In a microwave-safe bowl, microwave broccoli in a small amount of water for 3 minutes.

Serve salmon with sweet potato fries and broccoli.

INGREDIENTS

2 medium-size sweet potatoes, peeled and cut in thin sticks

2 tbsp olive oil, divided

2 salmon fillets (14 oz/390 g)

1 lemon, sliced

1 small onion, minced

4 cups (1 liter) broccoli florets

For the seasoning

2 tsp dried thyme, divided

Salt and black pepper

Nutrition Facts	
Per serving	
Amount	
Calories	310
Fat	14 g
Sodium	112 mg
Carbohydrates	30 g
Fiber	6 g
Protein	24 g

SCRAMBLED TOFU
with Broccoli

4 servings • PREPARATION: 10 minutes • COOKING TIME: 5 minutes

INGREDIENTS

1 lb (500 g) firm tofu

2 tbsp canola oil

1 onion, minced

¼ cup (60 ml) water

½ can (19 oz/540 ml) diced tomatoes, drained

2 cups (500 ml) broccoli florets

½ cup (125 ml) low-fat grated cheese

For the seasoning

1 tbsp garlic powder

1 tsp ground turmeric

1 tbsp dried basil

1 tbsp paprika

Salt and black pepper

METHOD

Using your hands or a fork, break up tofu into small pieces.

In a skillet over high heat, heat oil and sauté onion for 1 minute. Add tofu and seasonings and mix together thoroughly. Add water and tomatoes and mix together. Add broccoli and cook for 4 minutes. Add cheese and mix thoroughly until cheese is melted.

Serve with Tortilla Chips (p. 98) or 1 to 2 slices of whole-grain bread.

• • • • • • • • • • • • • •

TIP

Scrambled tofu is a nutritious way to replace scrambled eggs for breakfast, lunch or dinner.

Nutrition Facts
Per serving

Amount	
Calories	214
Fat	18 g
Sodium	241 mg
Carbohydrates	9 g
Fiber	2 g
Protein	22 g

MUSHROOM
Omelet

4 servings • PREPARATION: 5 minutes • COOKING TIME: 5 minutes

INGREDIENTS

8 eggs

¼ cup (60 ml) milk

¼ cup (60 ml) your choice of grated cheese

2 cups (500 ml) Paris or white mushrooms, cut in thick slices

1 red bell pepper, finely chopped

1 green onion, chopped

For the seasoning

Salt and black pepper

METHOD

In a bowl, using a fork, beat eggs and milk. Add cheese, mushrooms, bell pepper, onion, salt and black pepper.

Pour mixture into a heated nonstick or lightly oiled skillet over medium-high heat. Cook omelet for 2 to 3 minutes, fold in two and continue to cook to desired doneness.

Serve each serving with 2 slices of toasted whole-grain bread.

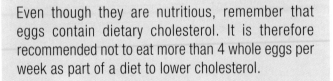

CHOLESTEROL INFO

Even though they are nutritious, remember that eggs contain dietary cholesterol. It is therefore recommended not to eat more than 4 whole eggs per week as part of a diet to lower cholesterol.

Nutrition Facts Per serving	
Amount	
Calories	324
Fat	12,5 g
Sodium	221 mg
Carbohydrates	7 g
Fiber	0 g
Protein	27 g

VEGGIE
Burgers

6 burgers • PREPARATION: 20 minutes • COOKING TIME: 10 minutes

INGREDIENTS

1 can (19 oz/540 ml) black beans, drained and rinsed

1 tbsp olive oil

1 cup (250 ml) cooked quinoa

¼ cup (60 ml) old-fashioned rolled oats

1 onion, minced

2 cloves garlic, crushed

1 egg

1 cup (250 ml) breadcrumbs

6 whole-grain hamburger buns

Your choice of condiments (mustard, ketchup, chutney, etc.)

For the seasoning

1 tsp ground cumin

1 tsp chipotle sauce

1 tsp dried basil

Salt and black pepper

METHOD

In food processor, combine black beans with olive oil and blend into a purée.

Add quinoa, rolled oats, onion, garlic, egg and seasonings and blend in food processor to obtain a consistent mixture without puréeing.

Transfer mixture to a bowl and add bread-crumbs. Use a spoon to blend thoroughly. Using hands, form ino 6 patties, about 1 inch (2.5 cm) thick.

In a lightly oiled skillet over medium heat, cook patties for 4 to 5 minutes on each side.

Fill hamburger buns with patties and your choice of condiments.

Serve with a green salad.

• • • • • • • • • • • • • •

TIPS

- Cook a batch of patties and store them in the freezer so you can prepare a good meal when pressed for time.

- Store cooked quinoa in the freezer for tasty and nutritious meals in the wink of an eye. One cup (250 ml) of uncooked quinoa yields 4 cups (1 liter) cooked quinoa.

Nutrition Facts	
Per burger without condiments	
Amount	
Calories	385
Fat	9 g
Sodium	416 mg
Carbohydrates	60 g
Fiber	8 g
Protein	16 g

BEEF
Noodle Soup

6 servings • PREPARATION: 20 minutes • COOKING TIME: 35 minutes

INGREDIENTS

9 oz (270 g) stewing beef,
cut in small cubes

2 tbsp unbleached all-purpose flour

2 tbsp canola oil

1 onion, minced

2 cloves garlic, minced

4 stalks celery, chopped

3 carrots, sliced

8 cups (2 liters) water

2 tbsp low-sodium beef bouillon
powder

1 cup (250 ml) small soup noodles

For the seasoning

1 tbsp dried oregano

1 tbsp dried thyme

1 tbsp dried tarragon

1 tsp dried rosemary

Salt and black pepper

METHOD

In a bowl, coat beef cubes in flour.

Heat oil in a large saucepan over high heat. Add onion and garlic and gently fry for 1 minute. Add celery and carrots and sauté for 1 minute. Add beef cubes and cook, stirring constantly, for 1 to 2 minutes.

Add water, dilute beef bouillon and add seasonings. Bring to a boil, reduce heat to medium-low and let simmer for 15 minutes.

Add noodles and let simmer for 15 minutes.

• • • • • • • • • • • • • •

TIP

This soup freezes well and can be heated in a microwave oven for a quick meal.

Nutrition Facts	
Per serving	
Amount	
Calories	290
Fat	12 g
Sodium	428 mg
Carbohydrates	27 g
Fiber	3 g
Protein	17 g

Quiche

6 servings • PREPARATION: 20 minutes • COOKING TIME: 1 hour

INGREDIENTS

1 tbsp canola oil

2 small onions, minced

8 eggs, beaten

1 cup (250 ml) milk

¾ cup (180 ml) unbleached all-purpose flour

1 tsp baking powder

½ cup (125 ml) feta cheese, cut in cubes

2 cups (500 ml) baby spinach leaves, coarsely chopped

1 large or 2 small tomatoes, sliced

A few leaves basil, chopped

METHOD

Position rack in middle of oven and preheat to 350°F (180°C).

Heat canola oil in a skillet over high heat. Add onions and sauté for 1 minute. Reduce heat and cook for 6 minutes.

Meanwhile, beat eggs with milk, flour and baking powder. Add feta cheese and spinach. Add cooked onions. Mix together well.

Pour mixture into a 9-inch (23 cm) pie plate and top with sliced tomato.

Bake in center of preheated oven for about 1 hour or until mixture has completely set. Garnish with chopped basil leaves before serving.

Serve with a green salad or Vegetable Salad (p. 131).

Nutrition Facts	
Per serving	
Amount	
Calories	195
Fat	15 g
Sodium	316 mg
Carbohydrates	20 g
Fiber	2 g
Protein	4 g

TUNA
Sandwiches

4 sandwiches • PREPARATION: 10 minutes • COOKING TIME: 5 minutes

METHOD

Preheat oven to 350°F (180°C).

Place 2 slices of cheese on one half of each hamburger bun. Place all buns (cheese-topped and plain) on a rack and broil for 5 minutes.

In a bowl, mix together tuna, yogurt, Dijon mustard and seasonings.

Spread tuna mixture on each cheese-covered hamburger bun and garnish with a lettuce leaf. Cover with plain half of bun to make a sandwich.

Serve each sandwich with ½ to 1 cup (125 to 250 ml) of your choice of raw vegetables (carrots, cucumber, celery, cauliflower, broccoli, etc.)

INGREDIENTS

4 whole-grain hamburger buns, halved

2 oz (60 g) Cheddar cheese
(8 thin small slices)

2 cans (3 ½ oz/105 g)
or 1 can (7 oz/198 g) tuna, drained

2 tbsp plain Greek yogurt

1 tbsp Dijon mustard

4 lettuce leaves

For the seasoning

1 tsp garlic powder

1 tsp paprika

Salt and black pepper

CHOLESTEROL INFO

• •

Tuna is a fish rich in omega-3 fatty acids, which are especially good for controlling blood cholesterol levels.

Nutrition Facts	
Per sandwich	
Amount	
Calories	340
Fat	11 g
Sodium	470 mg
Carbohydrates	30 g
Fiber	3 g
Protein	30 g

RED KIDNEY BEAN
Croquettes

4 servings • PREPARATION: 20 minutes • COOKING TIME: 10 minutes

INGREDIENTS

1 can (19 oz/540 ml) red kidney beans, thoroughly drained and rinsed

1 cup (250 ml) breadcrumbs

2 eggs

3 cups (750 ml) baby spinach leaves, coarsely chopped

1 tbsp Dijon mustard

10 Paris or white mushrooms, finely chopped

1 tbsp canola oil

For the seasoning

1 tbsp garlic powder

½ tbsp dried oregano

Salt and black pepper

METHOD

In food processor, purée red kidney beans. Add breadcrumbs, eggs, spinach, Dijon mustard, mushrooms and seasonings. Blend thoroughly for a few seconds until consistency is even.

Using your hands, form into 8 large croquettes. In a skillet over medium heat, heat oil and cook croquettes for 5 minutes on each side.

Serve with Tabbouleh (p. 106) or Vegetable Salad (p. 131).

• • • • • • • • • • • • •

TIP

These croquettes can be topped with homemade tomato sauce or served in a hamburger bun with your choice of condiments.

Nutrition Facts	
Per serving	
Amount	
Calories	330
Fat	8 g
Sodium	320 mg
Carbohydrates	46 g
Fiber	12 g
Protein	19 g

BARLEY AND CHICKEN
Pilaf

4 servings • PREPARATION: 20 minutes • COOKING TIME: 40 minutes

INGREDIENTS

1 onion, minced

2 tbsp olive oil

2 cups (500 ml) water

1 cup (250 ml) hulled barley

1 tbsp low-sodium chicken bouillon powder

1 clove garlic, crushed

1 tbsp canola oil

2 large boneless, skinless chicken breasts (14 oz/390 g), cut in strips

Zest of 1 lemon

2 red bell peppers, cut in pieces

4 stalks celery, chopped

10 Paris or white mushrooms, cut in pieces

For the seasoning

2 tsp dried thyme, divided

1 tbsp dried oregano

Salt and black pepper

METHOD

In a saucepan over high heat, sauté onion in olive oil for 2 minutes. Add water, barley, chicken bouillon powder, garlic and 1 tsp of the thyme. Bring to a boil, reduce heat to low and let simmer for about 30 minutes.

Meanwhile, in a skillet over medium-high heat, heat canola oil and sear chicken strips for 1 minute on each side. Reduce heat. Add lemon zest, remaining thyme, oregano, salt and black pepper. Add vegetables and cook over medium-low heat for about 6 minutes or until chicken is no longer pink inside.

Nutrition Facts	
Per serving	
Amount	
Calories	434
Fat	13 g
Sodium	250 mg
Carbohydrates	46 g
Fiber	11 g
Protein	32 g

CHOLESTEROL INFO

Barley can replace pasta in a variety of dishes and soups. It can also be added to desserts to increase the amount of soluble fiber in a recipe and thus help control blood cholesterol levels.

AVOCADO AND SHRIMP
Salad

4 servings • PREPARATION: 10 minutes

INGREDIENTS

2 ripe but firm avocados, cut in cubes

10 oz (300 g) cooked small shrimp

2 cups (500 ml) baby spinach leaves

1 cup (250 ml) red grapes, cut in half

1 red bell pepper, diced

1 tbsp olive oil

Juice of 1 lemon

For the seasoning

2 tbsp chopped fresh cilantro

Salt and black pepper

METHOD

In a large bowl, mix all ingredients together and serve.

Serve this salad with Tortilla Chips (p. 98).

CHOLESTEROL INFO

• •

The avocado is sometimes shunned for being high in fat. Contrary to popular opinion, it is an excellent source of good fat, soluble fiber and phytosterols that help to control blood cholesterol levels.

Nutrition Facts	
Per serving	
Amount	
Calories	250
Fat	15 g
Sodium	545 mg
Carbohydrates	16 g
Fiber	6 g
Protein	16 g

BAGELS
with Smoked Salmon

2 servings • PREPARATION: 10 minutes

INGREDIENTS

2 tbsp light cream cheese

2 whole-grain bagels, cut in half

5 oz (150 g) sliced smoked salmon

1 small red onion, slivered (optional)

For the seasoning

1 tbsp dried dill

Black pepper

METHOD

In a small bowl, blend cream cheese with seasonings.

Spread cream cheese on bagels and garnish with slices of smoked salmon. Add a few slices of onion if desired.

Serve with ½ to 1 cup (125 to 250 ml) of your choice or raw vegetables or Vegetable Salad (p. 131).

CHOLESTEROL INFO

Smoked salmon can be eaten as part of a low-cholesterol diet. Oily fish like salmon, whether smoked or not, is lower in fat than the leanest meats

Nutrition Facts	
Per serving	
Amount	
Calories	300
Fat	6 g
Sodium	800 mg
Carbohydrates	39 g
Fiber	3 g
Protein	22 g

GRILLED STEAK
Fajitas

4 servings • PREPARATION: 20 minutes • COOKING TIME: 10 minutes

INGREDIENTS

1 small onion, slivered

1 tbsp canola oil

11 oz (310 g) lean steak, cut in strips

1 tsp chipotle sauce or chili sauce

1 red bell pepper, cut in strips

1 orange bell pepper, cut in strips

4 large whole-grain tortillas

1 cup (250 ml) grated low-fat Cheddar cheese

½ cup (125 ml) salsa

1 cup (250 ml) chopped romaine lettuce

For the seasoning

1 tsp ground coriander seeds

1 tsp freshly ground black pepper

Salt

METHOD

In a skillet over high heat, sauté onion in oil for 1 minute. Add steak, seasonings and chipotle sauce. Sear steak for 1 minute on each side.

Reduce heat and add bell peppers. Cook, stirring frequently, for 5 minutes.

Fill tortillas with steak, bell peppers, cheese, salsa and lettuce.

Serve fajitas with Vegetable Salad (p. 131) or a green salad if desired.

• • • • • • • • • • • • • •

TIP

You can replace the steak with chicken.

Nutrition Facts Per serving	
Amount	
Calories	430
Fat	19 g
Sodium	650 mg
Carbohydrates	35 g
Fiber	3 g
Protein	30 g

GRILLED CHEESE SANDWICHES
with Apple and Chicken

4 sandwiches • PREPARATION: 10 minutes • COOKING TIME: 15 minutes

INGREDIENTS

1 tbsp olive oil

10 oz (300 g) boneless, skinless chicken (2 small breasts), cut in strips 2 inches (5 cm) long and 1 inch (2.5 cm) wide

4 oz (120 g) Cheddar cheese, sliced

8 slices whole-grain bread

1 green apple, thinly sliced

For the seasoning

1 tsp garlic powder

1 tsp dried thyme

Salt and black pepper

METHOD

Heat oil in a skillet over medium-high heat. Add chicken strips and sear for 1 minute on each side. Reduce heat to medium-low. Add seasonings and continue to cook, stirring occasionally, for 7 to 8 minutes, until chicken is no longer pink inside.

Spoon chicken and place cheese on 4 slices of bread. Add a few slices of apple and top with remaining 4 slices of bread.

Place sandwiches in lightly greased skillet and grill for 1 to 2 minutes on each side until cheese is melted.

Serve with Vegetable Salad (p. 131).

Nutrition Facts	
Per sandwich	
Amount	
Calories	424
Fat	15 g
Sodium	440 mg
Carbohydrates	33 g
Fiber	6 g
Protein	37 g

ABOUT
the Author

Alexandra Leduc is a registered dietitian, who graduated in biochemistry and nutrition from Laval University. She is the author of many cookbooks.

She is also the founder of Alex Cuisine (alexcuisine.com), a company that promotes health through healthy and fast cooking. In her classes, which include parent and child coaching and online videos, she presents simple approaches to everyday cooking.

What she loves most is creating delicious recipes with readily available ingredients. "You don't need to raid an organic food store or be a great chef to eat properly," she believes. Alexandra advocates an approach to cooking that is grounded in reality and is a long way from culinary competitions.

She also offers expertise in weight management and helps people develop a healthy relationship with food and achieve a balanced weight, while avoiding diets and restrictions. She has developed an approach — mindful eating — along with an online program (alimentationconsciente.com), which presents tools for applying it daily.

In 2011, she was named Young Business Personality in the professional services category by the Jeune chambre de commerce de Québec (Young Chamber of Commerce of Quebec). In May 2013, she received the Young Woman of the Year award as part of the YWCA Quebec's Women of Distinction gala, and in 2014, Laval University's Alumni Association named her Influential Alumnus.

alexcuisine.com
peplime.com

ACKNOWLEDGMENTS

Special thanks to my family and my husband, Jean-Philippe Sirois. I would surely not have accomplished this without you. Your unconditional support and encouragement make all the difference. Thanks to my mother, Christiane, who cheerfully tests and takes part in making these recipes. Your help is always so precious to me.

Special thanks to Modus Vivendi Publishing, Marc G. Alain, Isabelle Jodoin, Nolwenn Gouezel and all the team for your confidence in me and for the great projects you allow me to be part of; you make it such a rewarding experience. Thanks for helping people eat better.

I must also mention the work of photographer André Noël, whose magnificent photos always manage to whet the appetite.

RESOURCES
for High Cholesterol Sufferers

Heart and Stroke Foundation
www.heartandstroke.com

Canadian Cardiovascular Society
www.ccs.ca

National Heart, Lung, and Blood Institute
www.nhlbi.nih.gov

American Heart Association
www.heart.org

Mayo Clinic
www.mayoclinic.org/diseases-conditions/high-blood-cholesterol/home/
ovc-20181871

RECIPE
Index

KNOW WHAT TO EAT

A diet suited to your needs based on advice from expert dietitians

ARTHRITIS AND INFLAMMATION
21 DAYS OF MENUS
Elisabeth Cerqueira and Marise Charron, RD

BREAKFAST LUNCH DINNER SNACKS

BABIES
21 DAYS OF MENUS
Stéphanie Côté, MSc, RD

BREAKFAST LUNCH DINNER SNACKS

DIABETES
21 DAYS OF MENUS
Alexandra Leduc, RD

BREAKFAST LUNCH DINNER SNACKS

DAIRY-FREE
21 DAYS OF MENUS
Marie-France Lalancette, RD

BREAKFAST LUNCH DINNER SNACKS

IRRITABLE BOWEL SYNDROME
21 DAYS OF MENUS
Alexandra Leduc, RD

BREAKFAST LUNCH DINNER SNACKS

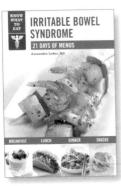

SPORTS NUTRITION
21 DAYS OF MENUS
Stéphanie Côté and Philippe Grand, RD

BREAKFAST LUNCH DINNER SNACKS

WEIGHT LOSS
21 DAYS OF MENUS
Elisabeth Cerqueira and Marise Charron, RD

BREAKFAST LUNCH DINNER SNACKS

CHOLESTEROL
21 DAYS OF MENUS
Alexandra Leduc, RD

BREAKFAST LUNCH DINNER SNACKS

MODUSVIVENDIPUBLISHING.COM